mosaics

Elizabeth Atkins-Hood  Elizabeth Joy Bell

A&CB

NOTICE TO READERS

For your safety, please use care when following any procedures described in this book. The Publisher and Authors assume no responsibility for any damage to property or injury to persons as a result of using this information. Always follow manufacturer's instructions and safety advice when using equipment or products.

First published in the UK in 2011 by A & C Black,
an imprint of Bloomsbury Publishing Plc.
49–51 Bedford Square
London WC1B 3DP
www.acblack.com

First published in New Zealand in 2011 by David Bateman Ltd,
30 Tarndale Grove, Auckland, New Zealand

CIP Catalogue records for this book are available from the
British Library and the US Library of Congress.

ISBN 978-1-4081-3133-6

Design Trevor Newman Design
Printed and Bound in China through Colorcraft Ltd, Hong Kong

Dedication

To the magnificent women in our lives — both friends and family — who help to get us through, in particular mums and grandmas.

Monica Sansbury Teare
Pamela Jeffs-Hood
Elsie Atkins-Jeffs
Lilian Boler-Hood
Betty-Lou Swanson
Olive Fennefos-Swanson
Sally Alexander

Also to Liz's dad, Ross Edward Hood, who we admire hugely for his zest for life.

Ruth Day

Life has its bonuses and fortunately for me it was to meet Ruth Day. Ruthie is a fully addicted, extremely clever mosaic artist.

It is because of Ruthie's belief in me as a mosaic artist that she asked me to write this book. Nearly three years later I am glad she did. Ruth's husband Pete added his ten cents' worth, stating that he wanted a coffee table book that even non-mosaicers would want to take time to enjoy. Thanks guys for initiating this project.

Acknowledgements

Acknowledgements to all the clever people who have influenced us along the way are made throughout the book, along with the piece associated with them.

Beyond our thanks to our publisher, David Bateman Ltd, a very special person needs to be honoured for her patience and ability to decipher chaos — Tracey Borgfeldt, our editor. She has managed to harness our artistic energy, a no doubt daunting task! Thanks Tracey.

Contents

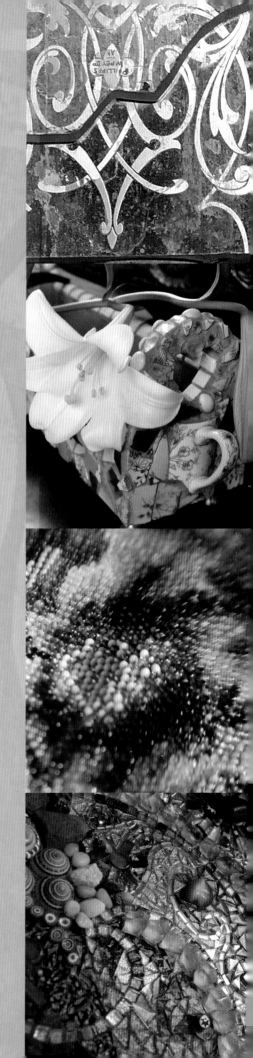

the authors

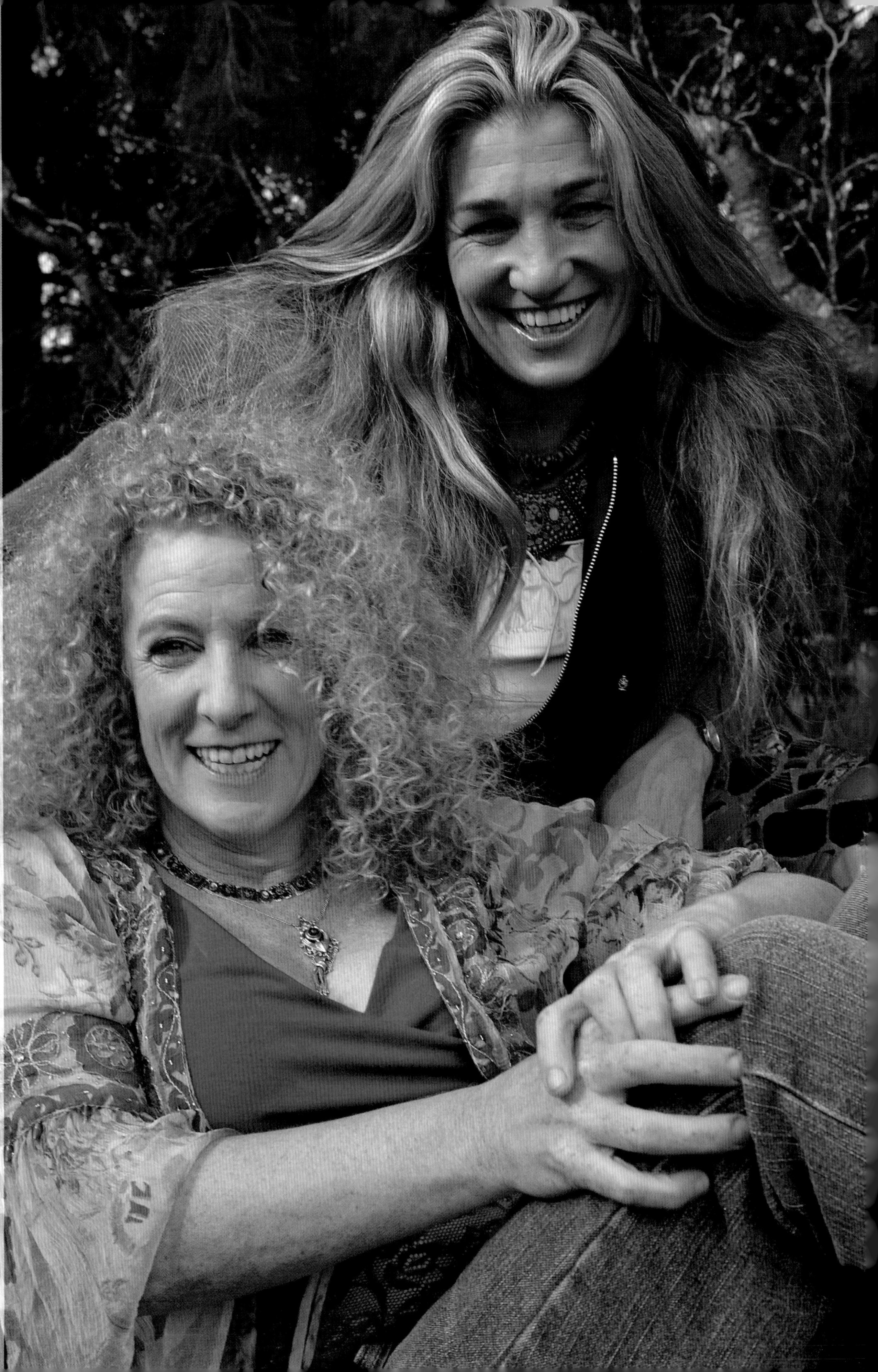

Hi, my name is Elizabeth Atkins-Hood. After 13 years abroad, I moved back from the U.S. of A. to my home village of Kaipara Flats, in the North Island of New Zealand — basically in the boondocks of nowhere. While in America, I developed skills as a mosaic and découpage artist. My passion lies in making something out of nothing, or transforming something sickly kitsch into an object of beauty.

Elizabeth Atkins-Hood

I started my creative life at five, when my dad taught me to knit. Even back then, I preferred to make up my own designs rather than following patterns. I was limited by the remnants of yarn I could afford to buy, which created boundaries in colour and design. I majored in art at school, which I was only okay at because I talked too much in class. I found that I really enjoyed tactile, more practical art experiences, so at eighteen I attended a night class on stained glass which launched me into that fantastic medium. I challenged myself by creating some quite complicated projects.

While living in the majestic mountains of Big Bear, California, I enjoyed learning the folk art of tole painting (also known as decorative painting). I realised that every new skill you acquire builds on your old skills and eventually they all end up relating to each other in your art. Recently, I have started fine art painting, and that is fun and very challenging!

Mosaicing encompasses all of the above skills (and more). I discovered mosaics after a visit 'down under' when my grandmother died. The scraps and junk under her house were the grandkids'

inheritance. That is where I discovered some old broken Crown Lynn cups and plates discarded in the corner. I decided to recycle them on an old lamp base to remind me of my grandparents. My next project was slightly more sophisticated: I created my first random china mosaic mirror frame as a gift for my girlfriend's wedding.

After meeting Jessie Cogswell and his phenomenal glass and tile saws (which you'll read about later in the book), I was off! Jessie's inventions were a catalyst to exploring and controlling shapes.

Meanwhile back in Kaipara Flats, I was flabbergasted to meet my neighbour Joy Bell, who is not only an extremely talented artist but, more importantly, her passion is mosaicing and découpage. It is too much of a coincidence! Consequently, when another mosaicing friend, Ruth Day, asked me to write a book, I immediately thought of Joy as co-writer, especially as our mosaicing styles complement each other. So, without further ado let me introduce Elizabeth Joy Bell and her story. Liz

ABOVE: This mosaic reminds me of New Zealand, with its kiwi centre. It is also reproduced on page 87.
OPPOSITE: Elizabeth Atkins-Hood (at back) and Joy Bell, Kaipara Flats, Northland, New Zealand.

When I was young, all I ever wanted to be was an artist. By the age of 12 I was selling my 'oils' in coffee shops. My dream was realised when I attended Fine Art School, aged 17, but then shattered when my art was ridiculed for being too technically orientated. I became a commercial artist by default, then opened an art gallery that became an antique store.

Elizabeth Joy Bell

For 12 years I was immersed in the ultimate treasure hunt... the acquisition, restoration and presentation of beautiful old objects. I then had a complete lifestyle change. I left the city, shop and a relatively carefree lifestyle to move into an old 1886 church in an idyllic rural community and raise my two young children. This gave me the opportunity to become an artist again – I was single and had to work from home.

My passion for mosaics began with 80 boxes of old china... chipped treasures, old cups, broken bisque figurines and mismatched Victorian tiles. These were the sad, unwanted leftovers of my well-stocked antique shop. I remember prior to moving to the country that I was going to dump these boxes. I wanted a clean break and to let go of my past. Instead, they were loaded into the truck and stored in a shed. This was to become a pivotal decision.

My first mosaic was an impulsive act – I slapped concrete over some blocks to make steps, suddenly remembered the boxes of china and naively embedded them. At the time I was unaware that

there was a huge revival in this ancient art form; that there were books, workshops, obsessive people forming societies and attending conventions!

The next step in mosaics for me were garden sculptures (see pages 46–53). I fell in love with concrete and used all sorts of recycled junk. I then hosted bus tours, inviting the public to view the sculptures. This brought clients into my studio and eventually the recognition to gain contracts for public art and beautification projects.

I am currently mosaicing the second side of my home (see pages 70–71) and exhibiting smaller works in galleries. Most of these works include the use of polymer clay — it's a fantastic medium for creating your own materials for mosaics and can 'capture' the designs and textures of objects without sacrificing them to the one mosaic. Joy

Above: One of my later works using found objects and polymer clay.
OPPOSITE: Detail of the steps with broken china embedded direct into concrete.

To motivate and **inspire mosaic artists** of all levels to keep extending themselves.

To share knowledge and our experiences through trial and error **to save you time.**

To share our **passion with others.**

To let you know that if you are **an obsessive compulsive mosaicist, you are not alone!**

Our goals

Deciding how to organise this book was a major task in itself. The mosaic medium is hugely varied, but after lots of discussion we decided that it was the materials that inspired us to create, so the main part of the book is divided into sections based on tiles, plates, glass, pebbles and rocks, polymer clay and found objects. While many of the projects featured use combinations of these materials, we've tried to choose those that particularly emphasise the benefits of the different media.

In this first part of the book, we cover some ideas about what a mosaic is and our thoughts on colour. We then look at the basic tools and techniques, especially the vital skills of gluing and grouting! The last section takes you through some projects step by step so you can gain the skills and confidence to tackle your own ideas and designs. *Joy*

Don't worry if you are an obsessive compulsive mosaicist, there are lots of us. One of our quests is to continue lifting the image of mosaicing above that of 'craft', and for it to receive the recognition it needs as a medium suitable for 'fine art'. Above all, it is loads of fun!

As this book has evolved, so has my desire to extend my own creativity to more 'outside the box' projects, so I guess it's working. Opposite is one of my absolute favourite mosaics, created by Rani Lange when she was only 17. Her inspiration came from a Vietnamese artist Hoang Thanh Vinh Phang. I was intrigued by her use of the subtle colour range of egg shells to create the contours of the face, along with other interesting choice of materials, including two varieties of leaf and the good old torn newspaper. I love the subliminal messages in the copy, especially 'GO FISH'. *Liz*

what is a mosaic?

A mosaic is... your own creative jigsaw of shape and colour. It can be uniformly patterned, pictorial or random but its goal is to be 'asymmetrically symmetrical' and give pleasure to the eye.

Mosaicing is a collection from thoughts to fridge magnets; pieces assembled in a particular way.

Knitting, needlepoint, quilting, découpage, and parquet flooring could all be considered to be mosaics.

OPPOSITE: Antique shoe lasts mosaiced with paper.

The most satisfying part of my mosaic journey is to give recycled materials that have had a former life another chance to shine. Pieces that have ended up on the scrap heap sit alongside treasures gathered from around the globe. They have equal importance.

What mosaics mean to us

This obsession we have for bringing fragments together and arranging them is universal. As the process progresses, it becomes addictive and takes on a life of its own. You follow an overall plan, but it still amazes me how the placement of a given piece can add or detract to the overall design and push you in new directions.

I am on a limited income and unable to afford material such as smalti (Italian glass tiles for mosaics). The wonderful thing about mosaics, however, is that the material you use can be proportionate to your income and start up costs can be negligible. For ten years, all I used to create shapes for my mosaics were tile nippers and many have only cost me the price of the adhesive.

As they say, necessity is the mother of invention and there is no shortage of sources of inexpensive materials, such as thrift stores and car boot sales. One of the joys of mosaics for me is the searching and scavenging for material. There is a potential gold mine around every corner; your imagination is the only limiting factor. Let the treasure hunt begin! Joy

Mosaic artists are people whose behaviour is similar to that of magpies — collecting, hoarding, sorting and categorising found objects. They then combine a cornucopia of recycled, bought or newly made materials into images and objects conceived from their busy imaginations.

Essentially, mosaic artists 'paint' with treasures, creating fine works of art that combine a cumulative array of artistic skills. Whatever the materials, from paper, tiles, smalti, china and even vegetables and fish! (see the next pages), there is definitely a process involved whereby the objects do the creating along with the soul of the artist.

The artwork eventually takes on its own life, to the point where your mosaic is partying on in its own groove! Even though you were the facilitator for the work, in the end the art piece has its own identity, with its own individuality, like a child of the artist. Once a mosaic is created, it is as if it has always existed. Maybe it has... in its creator's imagination. Liz

This 'Salad Eye' mosiac and the 'Vegetable Eye' mosaic, along with the 'Chocolate Eye' and 'Fish Eye', are fantastic examples of the diversity of material you can use for the art of mosaicing. Every mosaic takes time and these wonderfully creative, and

very different specimens, are the perfect pinnacle of this process with the use of yummy cooking ingredients and the 'catch from the sea'. The imagination of their creator is to be commended as the result is truly fantastic!

These mosaic images were created as part of a marketing campaign for New World Supermarkets in New Zealand. (Permission to use these eye images was kindly given by Foodstuffs (Auckland) Limited.)

Artists channel images. They are generally visual–spatial people who prefer to view the world in pictures.

For me, design and colour combinations rely on instinct. I like collecting together all of the product I need for a project (which is usually a lot), then I play and arrange it until something winky-wonky or quirky exposes itself, especially in the combination of shape and colour. At that point I start and let the mosaic take me on its journey. I am the guest!

The other pearls of 'left of centre' wisdom I have to share with you is what my mum, Pamela Hood, has always maintained... 'If you are unsure about whether two colours go together, take a walk in the garden. If nature has put them together then that is their validation, because nature's combinations can defy all rules of colour theory.' Look also at the contrasts in nature. Below is an icy cool, dynamic mountain scene in the South Island of New Zealand. Compare it with the fiery warmth of the sunset from our back lawn.

I have realised that mosaics need contrast to make the colours 'pop'. Often the grout acts as the contrast, which makes the choice of colour for the grout crucial. Black grout generally enhances colour in mosaics, but for what I call 'tone on tone' mosaics, where colours are within a similar tonal range, lighter grout colours work better.

Permission to photograph and include the fantastic colour wheel opposite was given by the artist Barry Sauvarin of Sauvarins Glass Room in Auckland. They are our local source of mirrored coloured glass and any other stained glass products and classes. As an aside, I recommend that all mosaic artists take a class in stained glass as glass and mirror are such dramatic mediums to add to your repertoire. Liz

What pleases the eye; what strokes the iris? What excites you and gives you that adrenalin rush? What sits together happily and does not argue?

Blues and greens are my personal favourites; they abound in nature, yet some say they should not be seen together. I have a dislike for primary colours, preferring the Victorian-style 'Persian carpet' look — rich, strong, sophisticated maroons, deep blues, lush greens. I have a very personal dislike for hot orange and reds (because they clash with my hair!)

I do try to limit my colour palette on each mosaic. Two or three colours with all their depth and tones will sit happier in a mosaic than trying too hard with too many colours. For the mosaics in my garden, I have tried to complement rather than compete with the natural beauty already there. However, if the site of the mosaic was a kindergarten, it would be more appropriate to use all the colours of the rainbow.

Similar art forms, such as knitting, needlepoint, stained glass and quilting, take a similar approach to limiting the colour palette. Less can be more. Joy

Thoughts on colour

Permission to photograph and include this fantastic colour wheel was given by the artist Barry Sauvarin of Sauvarins Glass Room in Auckland. They are our local source of mirrored coloured glass and any other stained glass products and classes.

Over the years, I have come to realise that I love to 'match' things – shapes, objects, designs and especially colour. As we are talking about 'nature-inspired' colour, I had to match these images from nature to mosaic pieces. I am so stimulated and driven by my obsession with colour that I am always observing and 'matching' my environment, and reflecting that in what I collect.

I feel the need to remind myself of the intriguingly dramatic, varied and simply unique environment that we live in. Even old junk can look fantastic nestled in wildflowers. Nature is the winner for warm, fuzzy feelings and as a source of inspiration time and time again. Lie on your back, let the sun warm your face and bask in the world of meditation, relaxation and imagination. Take the time to create.

The photographs on the right celebrate the colours and textures of nature. Liz

Nature-inspired colour

Creativity needs time, a clean brain and space to develop in.

Taking time to
**breathe in
nature** and
appreciate it
**will open the
channel to your
creativity.**

5/10 Taranaki River

Marshall Lefferts 2005

Outstanding photographer and now mosaic artist Marshall Lefferts has graciously let us include one of a series of mosaic photographs portraying majestic scenes of New Zealand. This particular image is Mount Taranaki in New Zealand. Originally inspired by David Hockney, Marshall toured New Zealand photographing scenes he later composed into mosaics. This composition is just one of the answers to the question, 'What is a Mosaic?'

Tone on tone

As much as I am addicted to colour, we can never forget about the extreme beauty of tone on tone, white on white or black and white. Throughout the process of creating this book, I have done a collection of these tone on tone mosaics, and generally they are the most popular. Perhaps it is because of their simplicity of colour, creating a clean, crystal, pure quality that soothes our souls.

Monochromatic colour is the variation of lightness and saturation of the same colour, which is generally very clean and elegant, especially when you experiment with the neutrals. I call it tone on tone and it usually lacks strong contrasts, as you use tints, shades and tones close to the base colour.

My favourite 'neutral' colour way includes gold, bronze, silver and pewter in all their variations often enhanced with

off-whites and blacks in spirals or blocks. I also like playing with opposites, for example black and white, using them to give the effect of strong contrast or to merge into each other to create shades of grey. The photo above (far left) does this, creating a mosaic around an illustration of Apollo on his chariot pulled by, originally, golden horses by artist Douglas Smith.

All colour schemes need to create enough harmony to be interesting to the eye. Once again, that is why I play with my product choices before placing anything. By moving them around they seem to select their own ideal complementary pieces, textures and colours creating a total visual seduction.

This photograph of an old tree by our local railway line is one of my favourites. The dramatic effect of the sweeping lines and the form of the sparkling tree could easily be the home of Forest Folk.

Under the tree are dew-laden spider webs. This photo demonstrates the perfection and beauty that is nature. This whole world in the early morning is so silent and seems so private.

Ruth Day created this neutral-toned bust to complement the concrete block wall in her garden. Simplicity of shape, form, style and colour are the essential ingredients of this mosaic's effectiveness. (PS: Spot the 'tattoo'!) Liz

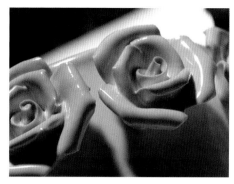

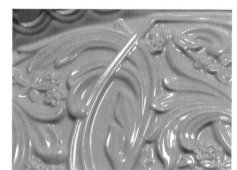

This mosaic mirror frame and the collection of plates around it demonstrate the interdependence of texture and minimal tonal changes that give this room its feeling of harmony and beauty. White on white mosaics are very elegant, and this approach crosses over to many styles of interior design — from Cape Cod, Shabby Chic, Victorian to Modern Chic. Neutral mosaics are soothing and stand the test of time.

White on white

When I lived in America I used to create with Gina Cerillo; she taught me how to découpage and I taught her how to mosaic. She is the one who first began making pure white mosaics. I have not managed to create a pure white one yet as I just can't resist the introduction of colour, even if it is only a slight tonal variation. In the mosaic mirror frame I *had* to introduce 'silver' in the form of the stars, which happen to be serviette rings that I sawed off keeping half the metal ring at the back so they would remain raised to the level of the thick tile.

Most of the luscious tiles in the frame came from over-runs from Ken Mason Tile in Long Beach, California.

The photos opposite are detail shots of either the plates on the wall or the mosaic. The beautiful angel plate came from a garage sale, the angel at the top of the mosaic came from Ken Mason Tile, as did the ribbon of tile beneath it which I cut out with my Gemini glass and tile saw.

As magnificent as the end result is, I struggled when placing the 'filler' tiles, that is the tiles that make up the bulk of a mosaic, especially as in this case they were quite plain. Liz

Mosaicing is like **creating an entity.** Its essence is the **pure joy of it. Turquoise and red** are my **favourite colour way...** from the **beginning of my life** until the end.

Turquoise and red

In this interior the colour palette is turquoise and red (one of my favourite colour combinations) with an accent of apple green in the frame of the mirror you can just see reflected in the mirror above the bed. I just cannot help myself either making or collecting pieces that match, especially in this colour combination. Technically speaking this is called a triad or tetrad colour scheme, which means selecting three or four colours evenly around the colour wheel (see page 21).

Within the concept of 'matching' though, it is fun to achieve a twist of funk, which is like an accent colour or something unpredictable or asymmetrical, something that is askew or 'winky-wonky'. In this context, the word 'match' also means 'balance'. I call it creating asymmetrical symmetry. The goal is to create harmony that encourages a swirling path for your eye, so you can take in everything. That is why composition is so important. I still prefer to rely on my instinct and I ask Joy if I am stuck. Liz

getting started

The mosaic medium is time-consuming, physically difficult and often unpredictable. Any tools to make this process easier are to be welcomed! Of course, many mosaics can be created with existing 'pieces' of tile, pebbles, and objects, but you will soon want to create your own pieces, and you need tools to do this. Having the right tools and materials to hand is important in getting the best result you can and avoiding frustration. The right tools will speed up the process and give more definition and detail to your work.

Tools

This section of the book covers the technical process of creating mosaics — the right tools, the right adhesives, the best substructures and grouts, plus lots of tips on getting your technique right and avoiding problems (look for these throughout the book — where we have encountered problems on a project we've tried to include solutions so you can avoid them!)

Hammers

Hammers are a great way to get started. Be sure to cover the tile or china with an old tea towel to control the shards. Then you can create wonderful crazy paving effects by fitting the random shapes together.

It is important to give yourself a border before you start so that you can control the outer edge. This technique is useful for large background areas. Start by using all the accidental straight lines that you can find for the outside edge and then simply fill in the rest.

Nippers

Nippers are an old metal tool used to dictate a crack. You apply pressure on the edge of the tile or china and angle the nippers towards the desired path. Most importantly, the nippers barely extend onto the material. This means that your control and angles are subtle and lots of

practice is necessary. You can 'nibble' a circle, but it is nearly impossible to indent a half moon shape. There are lots of 'miss-cracks' along the way and good humour is recommended!

Tile scorers

Tile scorers work like a glass cutter in that they scratch the glazed surface and pressure creates the break. They only work for straight lines and strip lengths of tile into various thicknesses over the 3 cm (1.2 inch) minimum. They are great for borders and linear effects. Strips can then be nipped or scored easily into squares and then into triangles or other less symmetrical shapes.

A lever is dragged over the tile and then returned to the start, and a small amount of pressure pops the tile in two. I call them my zip-zap machines and they come in different sizes based on wall or floor tile dimensions and are generally inexpensive. This is the quickest way to make a straight cut, but only works on tiles that have a flat surface. There is a tool that is handheld which has both a scorer and a plier action.

Tile saws

Tile saws come in two main categories: radial saws (of which there are many), which give you a straight cut, and

TOOLS TIP

Just as the tile saw uses water to protect the longevity of the diamond-encrusted blades, you need to protect the diamond bits on an engraver. Without water they will wear out quickly. Find a large plastic tray and submerge the piece of tile to be engraved. It seems strange at first working underwater but it takes only a small amount of water to benefit the bits.

Gemini ring saws, which create curves and shapes. There are different types of ring saw and choosing which one to use depends on the material you are cutting. These ring saws were invented and are manufactured by Jesse Cogswell for artists like himself. The Taurus ring saw is used for glass or wall tile shaping and cuts with a wire 'blade'. The Revolution XT ring saw uses a sintered blade and can create shapes out of much thicker and harder material (see next page for more detail about how these saws can be used).

Engraving tools

The most well known brand of engraving tool is Dremal. For the best results, you need to use diamond bits, which don't

TOOLS LIST

Hammers, nippers, scorers, tile saws, glass cutters, engraving tool, pliers, adhesives, grout, grout sealer, paint brushes, paper towels, sponges, safety glasses, gloves, tweezers and toothpicks, palette knife, craft knife, spatulas and masking tape.

As well as tools, you need the right adhesive matched to the right substructure — this will keep your mosaic looking good for years. The final element in most mosaics is the grout. Grout 'brings the picture into focus' and can have a harmonising or contrasting effect depending on what you are wanting to achieve. Grouting also keeps your pieces tightly and securely together: the ultimate aim for any mosaic artist.

come standard with the tool. Any motor is fine, but it is worth spending your money on a good bit. These tools allow you to add detail and texture to your mosaic, and you can even sign your name. An engraving tool can also mean you don't have to cut out tiny pieces.

TOOLS TIP

It is best to squeeze the nippers at the end of the handle to achieve a long lever and the strongest pressure – this will help you avoid RSI, or carpal tunnel problems.

... I haven't **nibbled for years** — but I nibbled for 10 years before that! Joy

The 'Revolution'

The Revolution XT, along with the Taurus 2 and Apollo, are part a series of glass and tile ring saws invented by glass artist Jessie Cogswell under the brand name Gemini Saws. Once you have opened yourself up to their omnidirectional possibilities, the creative world is your oyster. Liz

TIPS & TRICKS

When using saws that have a water trough, it is difficult to mark your cutting line without it washing off. Regardless of whether the marker is permanent, it will not hold onto the glaze without first being swiped with a dab of petroleum jelly or lip balm.

TIPS & TRICKS

If your plate is really hard, take your time with the saw. It will get through — I have even cut rocks in half with it.

One of my favourites sources of mosaic product are the HomeGoods stores in America. There, I find lots of plates and cups with particular themes, especially horse themes (which I love). The plates are often Spode, or other well-known quality brands. The animal and angel tiles I use a lot are from Ken Mason Tile in Long Beach, California.

I use the Revolution saw to cut anything I want to use for my mosaic from the plates or tiles. The saw can be used with its stabilising blade cover, or without when you need to cut large pieces.

All of the new plates or cups I purchase I put into general use in the kitchen. I always feel more comfortable cutting something up once it has a chip in it!

The brown horse below is being cut using a Gemini ring saw. I knew it was exactly what I needed to tie together a mosaic project I was working on. You may notice the horse's green ear. I have remodelled the broken ear with an awesome product called 'green stuff' (aka Kneadatite), a room-temperature curing epoxy which mixes blue and yellow components (hence its green colour). It adheres to ceramic, stone, wood, plastics, metal... almost anything you would ever need it to stick to! Eventually, I will paint it to match the horse's body.

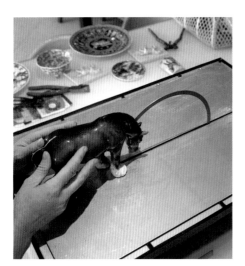

ABOVE: The horse form above was bought from an antique shop and it got repaired a few times before I got my hands on it to cut it in half. It is an economical way of using your product — you get two shapes out of one.

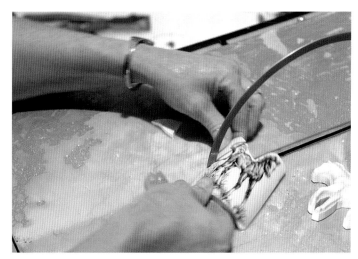

1 To take images from the sides of cups, cut down the sides of the handle and cut off the bottom. Then just cut around the image.

2 There are lots of great images I can take out of this plate. The cut-out horse on the table is from a tile.

3 I carefully cut into the plate to get to the central image and then around I go.

4 I retrieve all the other significant images from edges of the plate.

5 The border is also cut out as you can use it again as a border or randomly. I then nip the border into desired lengths.

6 After I have retrieved all the significant material from the plate, I just nip the remaining mini-pattern.

Substructures

Substructures are just the term for the base that your mosaics are adhered to.

Internal substructures
include:

frames
trays
teapots
vases
lamp bases
wooden boxes
plywood
paper-mache
drawers
doors
splash backs
pots
shoe lasts
busts
... and any rigid material

External substructures can be:

terracotta*
pavers
brick
polystyrene**
wire**
cement board
plastered walls
metal
... and any rigid material except wood. Wood moves too much and even marine ply can warp.

* Terracotta should be sealed with a diluted P.V.A. application.

**Polystyrene can be skinned with a mortar mix or the cement adhesive. Wire needs the same skin treatment.

Adhesives and grout

The durability of your mosaic often depends on your choice of adhesive and compatibility with the substructure. If in doubt, ask questions of experts in the building trade or your hardware store.

There are three major types of adhesive:
- acrylic adhesives
- mortar and cement-based adhesives
- construction adhesives and epoxy resins.

The acrylic adhesives include P.V.A. (white craft glue) right through to multipurpose latex-based tile adhesive, also called mastic. These are used for interior mosaics.

Mortar is a combination of sand, cement and water. Mortar mixes are called 'thin set' when used to adhere glass, stone and ceramic in a mosaic because a relatively thin amount is required compared to the heavier mortar used for bricklaying, for example.

Mortar should be used in the same consistency as thick mud (a small amount of P.V.A. can be added to the mixed mortar to strengthen the bond).

Cement adhesives are mixed with water to the same consistency as thick mud and are similar to mortar but with superior adhesion and convenience.

Epoxy resin is a two-part adhesive useful for metal bases and adhering figurines or found objects to your mosaic. It is strong, dries quickly, and is clear, but it is also expensive. Some, such as the Crystal Clear® series, are designed for projects that have to have absolute clarity. This adhesive is an exterior glue that is also flexible and it will move with the substructure. It can also be used on interior pieces where you want a thick but clear glue.

For larger applications, general-purpose **construction adhesives** are strong, inexpensive alternatives. They come in cartridge form and can be used for interior and exterior mosaics. (NB: Polystyrene melts in contact with these chemical adhesives, so use an alternative if working with polystyrene materials.)

Choosing the right adhesive

It is important to choose the correct adhesive and keep it compatible with the substructure. Also keep in mind whether the mosaic is indoors or outdoors. When you start to experiment with different glues, your preferences will emerge.

My favourite glue for exteriors is the ASA Superfixall cement adhesive — this concrete-like powder is mixed with water in an ice-cream container. I aim for the consistency of thick porridge. This enables the pieces to be levelled out as I place them and they don't slide around. If the mix is too watery, the pieces will not stay put and will 'slump' into the adhesive.

I have a preference for using construction adhesives for my interior mosaics. Usually associated with the building trade, these cartridge and caulking gun applications are also great for the craft person, and economy is only one of the advantages. Construction adhesive has a dependable consistency — when you push the glued piece down it doesn't 'cave in' — it holds its own. So I am continually gauging the amount

of glue needed to compensate for the thickness of the various pieces (having a flat surface in the final mosaic allows the grout to flow well and evenly between different materials).

When using the cartridge gun on delicate interior pieces, transfer a dollop of glue to a disposable sheet. Then work with a toothpick — twirling the thick glue to a peak. The toothpick keeps your gloved fingers off the mosaic.

The other advantage of this strong, thick adhesive on otherwise delicate artworks is its ability to 'skin over'. When it comes to cleaning up the residual glue, instead of a smear the 'skin' can be picked off in its entirety with a clean toothpick.

Choosing the right grout

When choosing your grout, read the instructions on the package with regard to the width of the gap you want to fill. Also consider whether your mosaic is outside or inside, and whether standing water may be an issue, as in a bird bath.

Heavy-duty grouts have a lot of sand in them, and are called sanded grouts. There are pros and cons to using

A range of adhesives for different jobs (from left): Superfixall (a cement adhesive), putty (used for embedding objects, see memory vase on page 119), premixed mastic (a latex-based glue), Aquadhere (a P.V.A. adhesive) and cartridges of construction adhesive.

them depending what you are mosaicing. Grout additives can be used to make the grout more flexible or able to be used in underwater applications. It is worth taking the time to make sure you are getting the product you need. If you live in a cold climate, think about frost when choosing your grout product for outdoor mosaics.

There are also grouts that are much smoother and denser in colour than the sanded grouts. These can work better with more delicate indoor mosaics or where you want a smoother finish outdoors, or a strong colour. I am not big on using colours in my grout, preferring to stick to the blacks, greys and whites.

Adhesive as grout

I use the cement adhesive as grout when I want the exterior mosaic to be maintenance-free. Grout is the only part of a mosaic that will break down with time. Public art panels get cleaned with water blasters, so by using the adhesive as the grout the panel is totally durable. Also courtyard floors need to be solidly constructed. And if you use black grout it will become grey as it inevitably fills with dust and dirt.

Grout options (from left): Sanded grout (economical for large exterior projects), Superfixall (Joy uses this both as an adhesive and a grout), examples of coloured and white interior grouts and some essential grouting tools.

Gluing

The example of gluing opposite is on an interior wall-mounted 'cross'. The substructure was cut from plywood and therefore I used mastic — a white latex-based adhesive — to glue on the mosaic pieces.

You can apply glue with a toothpick for very small mosaics or precious pieces, or use a plastic knife or a regular old butter knife. Or you can squeeze the glue through a cut corner of a plastic zip-lock bag just like an icing bag; use surgical gloves or just use your fingers. I generally start out well-behaved, with my hands protected, but something generally goes awry and my hands suffer again.

I like to take time to create mirrored edges so that light can reflect off them and dance on the wall. Gluing edges on mosaics can get a little tedious — the pieces are hard to hold in place and they need constant readjustment while they are drying so they stay straight and square. A 'lazy Susan' really helps but you can just use cans to hold your piece above the workbench or table.

You can glue an area first and then press your pieces into it if you have them all ready, or you can use your butter knife or tool of choice to apply enough glue to the back of each piece and place them individually.

Do not over-glue. If you use too much, the glue will fill up your grout channel with the potential to end up all over your tesserae and make a mess. If the grout channel is filled with white glue and you plan to grout in black, you've just made a whole lot of work for yourself.

And don't under-glue, because if you use too little you run the risk of your pieces becoming dislodged during grouting. Then you have to glue and grout at the same time. The optimum amount of glue is equivalent to a generous spreading of butter on toast (which I why I often use an old butter knife when gluing).

Press the pieces down firmly, with a little wriggle into position to check the glue is doing its job.

It takes a bit of trial and error — and patience! When you mosaic, you have to think ahead. When gluing, you have to be thinking about and preparing for grouting. Gaps cannot be too wide, grout channels need to be clean and open, levels of product need to be reasonably even (unless you have planned otherwise). Pieces need to be securely glued and you need to consider how your grout will work on the tips of pieces and stepping down from the face of a mosaic to its edge. In this example, I created a 45 degree angle with my grout to bridge the top tiles and the side tiles. This creates a neat and uniform line around the edge of the mosaic, defining its shape.

PS: Every time I grout one of the delicate mosaics a piece always falls outs. See the next section on grouting for the solution to this perennial problem.

TIPS & TRICKS

When working on outdoor mosaics using a cement adhesive as the glue (and, perhaps, later as the grout because of its durability), clean if off within 24 hours. Even on glazed surfaces, the difference can be between the effortless wipe of a paper towel and the chiselling off of unwanted residue.

Another tip for cement adhesive is, if you replace a piece of tile use new adhesive as it has a memory after about 10 minutes.

1 You want to achieve a 45 degree grout angle from the flat surface on top to the flat surface of the sides.

2 The white border tile helps the gradual step-down effect, bridging the height gap between the travertine and the mirrored edge.

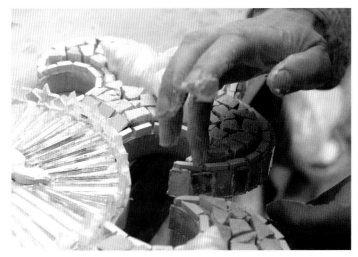

3 Elevate the mosaic on tin cans or, better still, a 'lazy Susan'. You can then spin your mosaic freely to work on it at any angle.

4 Focus on gluing the centre first and then each arm sequentially to ensure you are not reaching across your work.

5 The points need to be carefully managed so that the grout can successfully bridge the gap and stay put.

6 Gluing anything on the edge of the plywood takes time and patience. Keep adjusting the ones that slip a little.

Grouting

Grouting is a messy business, therefore you need a lot of newspaper or plastic underneath your piece; it needs to be elevated on tin cans to access the edges and you need grout, sponges, a paint brush, water for cleaning and paper towels.

Follow the manufacturer's instructions to mix the grout correctly. If it is too sloppy, it will cause cracks as the water evaporates from the grout. Too dry is better than too wet.

I prefer using sanded grout as it bridges a larger gap between your tesserae than non-sanded grout. Non-sanded grout is very tacky to work with and only bridges a gap of about 2 mm (0.08 inch), which is more suitable for miniature mosaics. Sanded grouts can bridge gaps of about 4 mm (0.16 inch), and even up to 10 mm (0.4 inch) in extreme cases, such as around the edge of an inserted plate.

Wearing gloves to protect your hands, massage the grout carefully into all of the grout lines on a manageable area. For this mosaic, I began with the centre section, then each individual arm of the 'cross'.

Once the grout is well buried in all

of the cracks and channels, covering all of the tesserae at this stage, it is time to start wiping off the excess grout with a damp sponge. The optimum is for the grout to be exactly even with the level of the tile or tesserae, not sitting above or concave between. It is a slow, careful process and patience is required.

Rinse your sponge repeatedly and continue wiping. Paper towels also help to remove excess grout. Sometimes I get the bulk off and then let the grout dry a little before I buff off the remainder with a shoe cleaning brush.

Well after the grout has dried, you can use glass cleaner for optimum shine, especially for pieces of mirror (but don't use too soon as I have had it leave a white residue when the grout has not been absolutely dry).

As a rule, I don't bother sealing interior mosaics, especially if they are hanging on a wall. The only times I would are when the mosaic would be subject to a lot of dirt or grease, such as in a kitchen or near a fire hearth, or when a particular material in the mosaic required it. For example, in this case, I sealed the travertine, which is a very porous marble, with special stone sealer to protect it from dust and grime and give it a little sheen. If I do this, I generally use the same sealer over the grout as well so the mosaic has a uniform shine.

TIPS & TRICKS

Masking tape is great for keeping grout away from where it should *not* be: on shells, unglazed tile, relief areas, polymer clay and any other breaks or cracks you don't want to draw attention to.

1 Elevate your piece on tin cans on lots of newspaper, as grouting is messy.

2 I generally always loosen a piece when grouting. You can reglue it in again and then carefully put grout around it (see 3).

3 By putting grout around your reglued piece, as the grout dries the glue also dries underneath.

4 I usually use gloves, especially to put on the bulk of the grout. The alkali in the grout really dries out your skin.

5 On big projects I use big sponges. On this smaller, more detailed piece, I am using a sea foam make-up sponge.

6 An old paintbrush can help to expose the detail and get into all the nooks and crannies. Use paper towels to wipe off excess grout.

7 I even used a toothbrush to help with the step down 45 degree angle on the edge of this piece.

8 A brush can also help buff off the excess glue and grout on the mirror and tile. Soft shoeshine brushes are good at the very end.

9 I carefully turn the piece over, protecting the tips of the finished side by using something soft on the tin cans.

10 I grout the back edge so it is smooth and glue on a large plate hanger. I use small screws to make it all extra secure.

11 The travertine needs to be sealed as it is a porous stone. This is a great product for a professional finish.

The finished piece mounted on the wall.

creating with tiles

Tiles are the mainstay for many mosaics, and are often the first material new mosaicists work with. As well as being economical, tiles come in various pre-cut sizes, uniform thicknesses and can be glazed or matt. The tile itself can vary from soft red clay to simulated stone flooring. As a lover of many different tesserae, I still use tile in nearly every mosaic I do. The flat colour of tile sets off the busyness of glass and china and the uniform surface works when you need it, even on 3D sculptures.

OPPOSITE: Paper-mache bust forms mosaiced in tile by Ruth Day.

Celtic crosses

The fake rock, decorated with glass flowers, with the Celtic cross on top is an extension of the mosaic wall nearby. It originated when a spa pool was removed and the concrete pad it was on remained. I liked the idea of a giant rock with a huge cross, so I assembled a heap of rubbish on the pad. Joy

Large items like washing machines, computers and other broken down household machines were gathered together and tied with wire. Polystyrene waste was pushed into the gaps as a filler, then green plastic sheets with a generous roll of chicken wire encased the rubbish. This was a free form mass so it did not need to be symmetrical or exact.

The next step was to construct the Celtic cross. This was made from a steel clothes hanger, padded out with polystyrene strips that were secured with wire. The cross was then liberally covered with a mortar mix and the detail carved out with a stick before the cement render dried.

The same mortar mix skinned the entire 'rock', once the cross was secured on top with wire.

Then the fun began, insetting a cast iron fireplace, with an old cemetery statue. The mosaic used to clad the rock was the same glass off-cuts, made into flowers, as on the nearby wall of the house. The background is a mix of free, simulated stone floor tiles.

This sculpture is literally made from recycled junk and it cost me three bags of cement. The trip to the tip would have been quicker, but would have cost more!

For smaller outdoor projects, use the same technique.

The mosaic used to clad the rock was the same glass off-cuts, made into flowers, as on the nearby wall of the house.

For both of these projects,
I used a cement adhesive
and a black grout.

Another obvious victim; the water tank (right) was just sitting there, minding its own business, collecting water, and the inevitable happened. Another mosaic cross!

This time a box of donated marble 'fingers' were used and in the centre a large cracked Royal Doulton plate. The background was simulated stone floor tile that was so heavy and hard to deal with that I smashed it with a hammer and used it like crazy paving. This, by the way, is a good technique for covering large areas of background.

The washing basket

This is my washing basket holder that services the washing line... no dryer for me. A round plastic bucket sits within what was once an old round washing machine 'drum'.

The bird was born when my young son walked past the boxes of unwanted bric-a-brac and pulled out a pair of chromed Art Deco wall vases. He stuck his hands in them and made out he was a bird — everything starts somewhere. Because I do not weld, I use a lot of recycled, found objects, tie them securely together with wire and then, as with the base of the bird's body, cover them with a cement mortar mix.

The galvanised drum was a good base because it will not rust and it has many holes, saving me having to drill where I wanted to attach other body parts. The neck is plastic down pipe, with the appropriate bend for the neck. I drilled and tied the beak to the plastic and then the pipe to the metal drum. The colander and tap were tied on for a bum. Two, once expensive Art Nouveau trays, were drilled and used as wings.

The four legged stand is heavy metal and the body sits balanced on top. The mortar mix was used only on the drum as the many holes provided a 'key' so that I could create bulk and roundness, without the mortar sliding off. The adhesive I use is cement-based and closely resembles cement. Most of my outdoor sculptures have a strong metal framework covered with a galvanised mesh form, then a mortar mix 'skin'.

The cement adhesive will attach securely to the metal (avoiding anything that will rust) and the plastic, the only prerequisite being that the base is rigid. Fibreglass also works well. For the bird we have two 1940s rubber feet, brightly tiled legs, plates, plaques, pottery and the tureen lids for the breastplates. The tile background means I don't need too much decoration. It has been incredibly useful for me to experiment with all these different components and test their durability in my garden.

The planter

My large 'jardiniere' in the garden came to be because this stand of banana trees never encroached onto the lawn. I mowed around them for years and it occurred to me that as they were so well behaved I could contain them.

I have always liked to play with perspective, placing big or small objects where they should not be or altering the scale of artwork. I wanted the banana trees to look like the aspidistra plants that the Victorians always had in their very ornate floral jardinieres.

I decided not to be overly concerned with a foundation or be too exacting with the circle. The main problem would be if the plants' growth pushed out the 'jardiniere'. However, although the weight of the side walls is minimal, it is heavy enough to support itself and the cement adhesive and tile adds more strength. The height of the pot is 1.5 m (5 feet) and I roughly staked out the circle with upright galvanised pipes hammered into the ground.

I then rolled wire mesh horizontally around the circumference twice. I used polystyrene boxes for the 'belly' and captured them at mid height by using the rolls of mesh vertically. This enabled me to get a good roll at the base and the top of the pot at the same time as positioning the polystyrene. Many short strands of wire were then used to securely tie all this mesh to the metal pipe.

The mortar mix was then slapped into and onto the mesh and over the polystyrene. This becomes a rather hit and miss affair, with a lot of mortar ending up on the ground.

The first layer of mix grabs the wire. Let that dry before adding the next layer, which will almost fill up the gaps. The third layer forms the skin.

I bought 55 mugs to get me the width of my top roll, and 25 flowers make up the floral band. The remaining background was any blue tile vaguely similar to the mugs.

The washing line

The washing line did not stand a chance... it was asking to be decorated. This is one ugly New Zealand classic, publicly airing your wet washing. They are cemented in fairly deeply so there is no movement to worry about.

I decided to create a brown pottery tree trunk with a coiling snake, eating an apple. My prime motivation was to make a shrine for my Victorian bisque Madonna. I am not a religious person but love all things related to churches.

I have used waste polystyrene for the free form shape and encased this in three layers of mesh. I then tied these together with wire and secured the form to the galvanised washing line. Old plastic irrigation pipe provided the snake and was duly wired to the mesh. An old enamel meat dish was recessed into the structure and tied into place by its handles.

The usual mortar mix was then applied. It is always a messy job, with more miss than hit as you valiantly try to pat the mortar onto the mesh with gloved hands. It falls through and off the mesh but eventually it all comes together to form a rock-hard skin.

As with most of my projects, I go with the materials at hand. Large pots curved with the snake and pottery gave the texture of bark on a tree.

In some places, where outdoor mosaics are affected by frosts, it is best to check with the manufacturer as some tiles might crack during the freeze/thaw cycle.

The sofa

The photographs opposite show the process of constructing a concrete garden sofa. The work and large amount of material necessary cannot be underestimated, but once you put it 'out there' that you are looking for stuff and keep your eyes open it is amazing what can be found for free. The most important criteria is not the cost but that you are happy with the result. You have to feel that it could not be improved upon five years later.

This sofa cost me 65 dollars, that is the cost of the cement and adhesive. What is not obvious is the preparation required for the pad that it is sited on. Without a solid foundation, the weight of this sofa would have caused subsidence and eventual cracking of the mortar mix and then the tiles would simply fall off. So a hole was dug and then filled with gravel, boxes of broken tile and glass (because they needed dumping) and then a decent load of cement, levelled off with heavy pavers.

The concrete blocks were recycled, and an unseen bridge of blocks supports the sheet of galvanised metal that forms the seat. After playing with the shape of the sofa (first photo), I then deconstructed it and reassembled the blocks, cementing them together.

Shaping of the rolled arms was achieved by using mesh; three layers were tied off with wire that was preset into the blocks. Then the entire form was liberally coated with mortar. I used gloved hands to pat it on, sometimes putting on three layers to create a firm skin over the mesh.

Then the fun started... I used only what was in the shed: plates, a tureen lid, odd tiles, some green mugs for the roll under the knee. The rest of the body of the sofa is what I call 'a rich tweed' of broken pottery. These pieces are usually mugs or jugs, richly glazed and, being curved, they follow the shape of the sofa nicely.

1 After the base was prepared, I experimented with the shape of the sofa using concrete blocks.

2 Once I was happy with the shape, I cemented all the blocks in place and used mesh and mortar to shape the arms.

3 The fun starts — you need to be sure you have all the materials you need before beginning.

4 Almost finished.

5 Cushion close-up. Tiles were a great filler for this project, covering large areas and providing a base for the plate details.

6 The finished sofa — the rear of which can be seen in the photo opposite.

Commercial work

Orewa is a seaside town north of Auckland, New Zealand. These high tech toilets needed to be attractive and reflect the feel of the town. One panel depicts pied oystercatchers, (wading birds often seen on the beaches of the region) and the other panel is the flower of the rewarewa, a native tree also special to the area. Joy

When making public mosaics, I prefer to work at home, so I purchase thick cement sheets that can be easily cut to size. This enables the work to be done flat without worrying about starting at the base and working up (as you would have to do if mosaicing a vertical panel). It is also much easier having everything at hand at home, and being able to stop and start when you want to.

I created the birds and the flower first, and then built the background around them. By this stage I had met Liz and nervously borrowed her amazing tile saw from America. I was able to cut out the birds' legs, beaks and some feathers as well as the flower's spiral stamens. This saw was a revelation to me! I had used nippers for ten years and it was a struggle to

create realistically and precisely. Needless to say, this commission paid for a saw to be shipped to me.

I used black grout to finish the mosaics as it gives a lot of impact. I hired two local builders to help me install the panels, which were both heavy and prone to damage in transit. It is always a bit nerve-wracking moving finished mosaics!

Puhoi toilets

The settlement of Puhoi originated with a ship that landed at a tidal stream in the 1860s. The settlers were from Bohemia and they brought with them a rich culture and a strong work ethic. Of great importance to this area was the kauri tree, the biggest of which were thousands of years old.

Their size and unusually straight trunks made them ideal for masts and milling. Thirty bullocks in paired teams were necessary to haul one massive trunk through ravines, thick bush and mud. The most intelligent animals were out in front and the strongest at the back!

Depicted in one of the two mosaic panels for this commission is Smokey, who with his mate, Lively, led a bullock team in the 1920s. Behind them is the kauri tree so important to the region and the estuary the settlers sailed up.

The other panel features the two most prolific native birds in the area, the New Zealand pigeon (left) and the tui, either side of a church window. For this panel, I used art glass for the river and floor tile for the light blue sky.

Once I have worked through the design and drawing phase, I start by getting my sketches enlarged at a photocopy shop (in this case twice). One copy is laid onto a cement panel pre-cut to its final size, and the other copy is cut into the pieces that I will glue with rubber cement onto the chosen tile. I then have many shapes, like the pieces of a puzzle, ready to cut out. I call this my sectiled method of mosaic; sectioning off various pieces that will make up the finished picture.

I then use a saw to cut around the shape. For softer tile, such as wall tile or glass, I use the Gemini Taurus saw and

for the hard floor tile I need the Gemini Revolution XT.

I was lucky enough to find some mottled grey fake-marble material in three different shades. These were invaluable in helping to create the illusion of animal hair. I was worried at the onset of this commission that I would be unable to give Smokey that soft look that a real animal has.

To help further with the fine detail, I purchased an engraving tool with diamond bits that cuts through the tile glaze. This allowed me to add some lines around the eyes, horns and chest of the bullocks and also the detail in the bird feathers. I could also write the text and sign my name. To darken these lines I rubbed in black permanent marker and to lighten the tui's throat feathers I used white correction fluid. I found that the engraver added another layer of detail, and it was very quick and effortless.

I never glue as I go, preferring to assemble all the pieces onto the complete sized-up photocopy first. I can then check for snugness and a relatively even grout line between each piece.

My material varies in thickness, from thin glass to thick fake stone floor tile, so I must glue the thickest material first to gauge my grout level and then bring each piece up to that level to ensure an even surface for the grouting stage. This is where a thick adhesive is a great help.

Wilson Cement Works

It may seem that I am the 'Toilet Queen', but I did do other public art jobs in between! What I have found is that the public commissions in these pages are a great indication of my progress as a mosaicist, both in technique and as an artist.

These two mosaic panels were commissioned by a council north of Auckland and installed in the new public toilets on an historical industrial site that includes a picnic area. The Wilson family were the first in the Southern Hemisphere to produce cement and the old ruins of the factory are the backdrop for a park and a popular swimming hole. The scow *Jane Gifford* serviced the area and transported cement as far away as Sydney. She is now restored and is moored a kilometre up the river, taking passengers past the cement works and out to the harbour. The family generously gifted the site to the public. (I always love doing the research and immerse myself totally into these public artworks.)

The cement sheets are cut to size and the many different varieties of tile are cut to shape using the Revolution saw. They are assembled in my shed and cement adhesive is used to level off the different thicknesses of tile.

A couple of pieces of tile are left off so that when the panels are installed onto the walls I can drill right through the cement sheet and into the cement wall and use anchor bolts to secure what is a very heavy panel. The spare pieces and the border are then affixed and the whole panel is grouted.

The challenge for me with these two panels was the detail required for the rigging on the scow and the buildings.

I used an engraving tool to add the rigging of the ship and the finer details

to the cement works. Engrave each piece as you go, before they are glued to the substructure, as you should ideally submerge each piece in a tray of water and engrave under the water. (The use of water dramatically reduces the wear on your expensive diamond bits.) The engraver can be powered by any cheap model motor, but it is worth using expensive bits — diamonds are the best

for breaking through the hard tile glaze.

I managed to cut out the sails in one piece out of large floor tiles; the fine detail of the ropes, creases and shadows were able to be added as a final touch. For the cement works panel, the ripples in the river, the bricks in the chimney and the old guy in the boat were effortless artistic touches with the engraver — it is just like using a fat pen (only permanent).

The council require these panels to be durable and maintenance-free. They also need to be completely flat, with no uneven surfaces. This is a public liability issue. Within these constraints there is still great scope for artistic expression.

Tiles are great as borders and fill in backgrounds quickly and effectively. For public art they are essential as the surface of public mosaics has to be level and smooth to the touch to avoid any public liability issues.

creating with plates

Romantic and
timeless, plates are like tiny
time capsules and can evoke
specific eras or places.
Recycling them into a mosaic is
the ultimate compliment for a
chipped or cracked plate, cup
or other . . . Their diversity
of colour and pattern is
unparalleled. And best of
all, they can be relatively easy to
source without great expense and
suit small and large mosaics.

Pique assiette*

Above (left) is a fun project that involved all of my young children. At the time, my five-year-old daughter loved drawing whirly-twirly butterfly flight patterns so we went, as a family, to a ceramic painting shop and each child painted a butterfly form with glaze. Liz

* A type of mosaic that uses broken plates and other ceramics.

Once fired, I created this little mosaic purse-hanger using the children's butterflies connected together with a curly, pebbled flight path.

I used pink paint with a white grout but it was not intense enough so I painted the grout bright pink.

Above are all-over floral teapots and shoe lasts covered in plates. Projects like these are deceptively easy, as it takes a

lot of planning to keep the shape of the substructure and follow the curves with the plate pieces.

The planter box above is a simple but satisfying project for the beginner. The planter box forms can be purchased from art and craft stores. Cup handles need to be recycled, too, but I wouldn't trust them as weight-bearing handles.

The thing I liked about this project was using draw pulls for the feet. I have used rose-shaped draw pulls in other work, so it is another item to keep your eyes out for.

Above (right) is Joy's very first mosaic — the steps up to her vegetable garden. Not knowing that a product such as a cement adhesive existed, she simply embedded the broken china and bric-a-brac straight into a slab of concrete. But

this has made no difference to the steps' durability — the pieces have stayed put through 15 years of hard use.

When placing the pieces into the bed of concrete, you have to keep going once you've started and there is no room for grout when the job is finished. However, the final result was practical, pretty and just goes to show there is more than one method that can work well.

For the love of plates

As a mosaic artist, it is not long before you have a collection of plates. I am truly infatuated with their variety and beauty; from complicated designs to the simple, striking colours. Liz

To me, there is a romance associated with their form or maybe it is the reflective quality of the glazes that transform light throughout the day or as they are pulled out of a sink of soapy water...

As I started my mosaicing addiction as a 'pique assiette' mosaicer, recycling old porcelain, china and other found objects, I have never really lost my love of plates. As time goes by, and minimalism is in vogue, Joy and I have had to wait for the next trend as we are both MAXIMALISTS! The plates on these two pages are from my sister Caroline's house and my own. Every plate is in the 'holding paddock' in case it might break and 'Oh shame,' I might have to recycle it!

As time goes by, and **minimalism is in vogue,** Joy and I have had to wait for **the next trend** as we are **both MAXIMALISTS!**

I have always considered **plates an inexpensive source of art** for our walls.

Mirrors

Why mirrors? I started creating mirrors in the late 1990s, as did a lot of mosaic artists. I continued because I never had my dream home and, as interior design is my passion, by creating mirrors I could always take my designs with me. I am a strong believer in putting together dream books so your designs ideas are always organised. I found that if I liked a design for at least five years then it had stood the test of time. Liz

Eventually, once I moved back to New Zealand, I did get my dream home and I have decorated most rooms around my mirrors. Now that my place of residence is permanent I am ready to start with bigger projects in the great outdoors.

To be honest I always found making mirrors economical; as the mirror itself takes up so much space you need less product for around the edges — therefore, you can use fancier material.

Mirrors with frames made of ceramic materials naturally lend themselves to use in bathrooms. The cute mirror far left was made from a series of pottery cups created by New Zealand artist Cynda Harris. They all broke on their journey to the U.S. so I created this mirror to remind me of home.

The elegant spiralled mirror next to it was created around a miniature cup and saucer I loved. I cut off the handle of the cup and sunk it into a hole cut into the ply base so it ended up more flush to the rest of the mosaic.

Glass is another ideal material for mirror frames. While living in Big Bear, California, a neighbour passed away and I was given his glass table and collection of glass pieces. Within it was the unusual petroleum glass I used in the frame above (left), along with pebbles, beads and ornaments.

Bulrushes, dragonflies and frogs, water lilies and rocks make up this little cutie.

The mirror above (right) is extremely quirky as the theme is frogs. The central découpage is of a frog wearing swimming trunks braving the elements with his umbrella. The image was from a Courtier greeting card from England purchased in Sonoma, California. Liz

It is always a compliment when you know that you as an artist have inspired someone to extend and develop their creative journey and in this case the inspirational credit goes to Cleo Mussi, one of Joy's favourite mosaic artists. The substructures for these mosaics are old ceramic meat platters, worked on their reverse side for a convex effect. A mastic adhesive was used to glue on pieces of plate, porcelain flowers, cup handles, shells and spirals of polymer clay. They have been finished with a black grout.

On the wall above is one of my even-sided, cross mosaics which has a découpage centre of a 1920s Chinese girl (detail right). Two of Joy's faces and my little Asian themed cross form part of the 'Blue Room' plate collection. Liz

Outside Joy's studio

This was an important job for me. The studio sits up proudly above my sheds and is readily seen. This was also to be the first mosaic ever for Jesse Cogswell, and his first return to art, after a 20-year hiatus.

I had met Jesse at the SAMA conference, thanks to Liz. Jesse was a sponsor and was demonstrating the amazing Gemini saws that he manufactures. We ended up great friends and he has since visited New Zealand.

So this was our first collaboration. Initially, we replaced the wooden boards with cement boards. I had returned from the conference with the resin head and the large green vase. We cut the vase in half and drew a mirror image of a vine. It immediately reminded me of Art Nouveau frontispieces in books.

With Jesse's formidable saw power we cut out approximately 400 leaves. We selected old plates decorated with gold or leaf designs. It is an education, watching Jesse cut with the saws that he has invented and manufactured for the last 20 years. Left to me the leaves would have been pretty mundane, but with Jesse's expertise the results dance exuberantly.

He has used the round edge of the plates to make the most of the gilded borders and some edges curl right off the wall. These could snag, so this fabulous textural quality cannot be used for art in public spaces due to possible liability problems.

The crazy paving background behind the vine really shoots the leaves forward. It is dark, rich and metallic. This contrast works well the opposite way too, with a light background amplifying a darker subject.

Above the green vases on each side are the words 'Waste Not, Want Not'. I took an impression from an antique platter with black polymer clay. The words certainly lend extra meaning to the mosaic, made up as it is from recycled plates that no one wanted. I will be interested to observe how the clay will weather. Certainly, a few years on, it looks perfect.

The gold glass tile surrounding the head above the door was the best available. It is in a very exposed position and I have had poor results from cheaper gold tiles used for exterior projects. The glass can part company with the backing.

When I step out of my house I am greeted with this vision — it is both beautiful and timeless. I believe it is important to surround ourselves with things that we believe to be beautiful; there is an undeniable feel-good factor to our aesthetic environment.

There is also a magical quality to some art that is produced, and usually it is accidental. The different shades of gold tile around the head appear to light up, especially in twilight or when there is no apparent light to reflect. And I am very pleased with the overall symmetry.

It is important to surround ourselves with things we believe to be beautiful.

Hitting the wall

This courtyard wall was my last available exterior canvas. I had two distinct needs to fulfil: a delicate, pretty pink and blue patchwork quilt effect and my compulsion to work crosses into everything. Plates provided the patchwork, with their myriad colours and designs giving a rich, textural feel. I did incorporate some floor tiles to create the background cross shapes so my stunning cast-iron crosses could be seen (see photo opposite). I haven't grouted my wall yet, but there is a small part where I have started which you might be able to spot in the photograph below. Joy

My home was once a church, so my **collection of crucifixes, rosary beads, crosses, icons and statues** are not misplaced.

I have an obsession with crosses and I am not sure where it comes from. I was raised a Catholic, so maybe it's from way back then. My home was once a church, so I feel that my collection of crucifixes, rosary beads, crosses, icons and statues are not misplaced.

In keeping with my obsession, my first art job was as an epigraphist — I created the epitaphs on headstones for a memorial stone masonry company.

I made my own headstone at the age of 19 — in case I ever needed one! Needless to say it will come in handy one day.

So it is no real surprise that I have covered one wall of my house with twenty large crosses with a patchwork quilt floral background. I also cut cross shapes out of tiles and plates with my ring saw. You can see the line I cut into the centre on the plate above (right).

However, one friend, who is an

accountant, did show some concern. She asked me if I had considered the possibility of my lowering the resale value on my home!

It has taken me 14 years to personalise this property, and I knew I was never leaving when I started this project. My reasoning is that it is a 'joy' not to have to consider someone else's tastes in pursuit of your own aesthetic vision.

creating with glass

Glass brings an intensity and depth of colour and light reflection to a mosaic — either as the main player or as an accent. Once mastered, the art of cutting glass is fast and universally useful. The range of colours and availability of coloured and textured mirror glass has expanded the medium enormously. Art glass can be used pictorially to create hills, sky and rivers elegantly. The added effect of mirrors and mirrored glass adds light and play as they reflect what they see.

Recycling antique mirrors

Old mirrors have a wonderful mysterious quality to them and I used a number of antique mirrors in this project. I needed to create a dividing wall in my studio, to hide the mess that I inevitably make from the clients who come to view the art pieces. Joy

A friend had visited Australia and recounted walking into a store that had an entire back wall covered in old broken mirrors. I was intrigued with this idea and knew that I had boxes of old advertising mirrors and round convex mirrors from the antique store.

I started by taking a hammer to a mirror that was incredibly thick and was disappointed to find that it wanted to break into dagger shapes. That was until I decided to recreate the old sunburst design that was so

popular in the 1960s and then the daggers worked a treat. I did no saw cutting and enjoyed the spontaneity of distributing the broken shards into an eye catching and mysterious montage.

The substructure is a large sheet of ply 1.3 m x 1.3 m (approximately 50 inches square) and 20 mm (¾ inch) thick. It is the same size as the large Victorian mirror that it backs onto. Both backs sandwich the voile curtain and make a room partition. They are supported by the sturdy desk that they

sit on top of and are kept upright by chains secured in the ceiling.

I glued the mirror pieces with a cartridge of the transparent Crystal Clear 202 and used a black grout.

I love the bust of Queen Victoria that sits in front of my mirror divider. I collect Victoriana and had always wanted a bust of Queen Victoria (doesn't everyone?). I made this one, and it took me 15 years. Surely a testament to the idea that everything gets finished eventually. She is huge and made from a recycled, headless

While sorting out my old mirrors, I discovered that some had very little silver backing remaining, like the shield bottom left. I found a faded image of a Victorian woman collecting shells from the beach and glued it image-side down to the back of the mirror... an interesting ghostly effect was created. This was then exaggerated by gilding the entire mirror.

The mixture of **silver, gold and bronze** is very pleasing to me; **I am a lover of all things old.** Nothing too shiny or primary in colour.

statue base, clay and plaster. Queen Victoria was in mourning for decades and always wore the veil and her brooch in memory of her beloved husband Albert.

I used old lace soaked in Mr. Stiffy for the veil and, behind her, spray painted through the lace with black onto the fake bronze finish. I used glass teddy bear eyes and gems for her jewellery and crown. I eventually located Albert's image, gracing the end of a clay pipe, took a mould from it, made a plaster copy and she was finally complete.

Découpage Joy's way

My gilded, reverse découpaged vases and plates echo the images and
the artists I admire.

Sometimes I feel like a time-travelling
thief, stealing images from centuries ago.
I particularly like Victorian images. I cut
out pictures that I want with a craft knife
and then glue them, image side, with 50
percent P.V.A. and water onto the glass.
Sponges are used to push air bubbles out
and to clean off residual glue.

To start, you need a clean glass vase
that you can get your hand into. And if
you want an overlaid effect you need to
remember that what goes in first will be
in the foreground. I have built up some
elaborate fantasy worlds... including
tropical, botanical and undersea themes.

Start off with a simple plan. The
danger is when the paper is wet and
fragile, as you can mistakenly rub it off
as you work alongside the neighbouring
image. Then, when the paper is dry it
really sticks onto the glass and is difficult
to remove.

Once all the images are glued
on, I daub on gold size with a large
paintbrush, completely covering the back
of the image and glass. Leave this for half
a day, it will not dry but is meant to stay
tacky.

For a vase, sprinkle in mica powder
(can be bright gold or old bronze) and
shake the vase until a very light coating
attaches to the gold size. Any remaining
powder can be shaken out and saved.

I leave this a day to settle in and
then pour acrylic polyurethane into the
vase. After rolling the vase around and
covering the gold completely, I pour the
excess off and save.

The vase should then be placed upside down on a plastic sheet for 10 minutes to ensure that the coverage is not too thick. This process should be repeated three times, drying the polyurethane between coats.

Before the last coat, I pour in and roll in the same way black acrylic paint (just once), and then finish with the third coat of polyurethane. The vase is well sealed, the work protected and the black hides the 'working' side of the découpage.

For a glass plate, the process is the same, though a little messier and lots of newspaper is helpful. The important thing to remember is to pour on that first coat of polyurethane as soon as you can because the gold size and powder cannot bear to be touched.

Another tip is that I always use ink jet photocopies for the images as paper from magazines shows through the type from behind and some computer copies fade.

Memory vases can be made using

photocopies of old sepia or black and white photographs. You can cut out the parts of the photos you want, or leave them complete and garland them with the person's favourite flowers and butterflies... it can be like scrapbooking on the inside of a vase. Gilded from behind, they can be charming, personal and very beautiful.

For more ideas see Liz's découpage on pages 88–89.

Recycled gilded vases

The bust I created (see next page) is the marriage of a $20 damaged shop display model and a broken box of gilded découpaged vases that I make. Vases were ideal as it would have been difficult to mosaic these curves with flat tesserae. The rose vases were well rounded and create a 'bikini'. The remaining body is made up from a delicious mix of gold glass tile and some shards of clear glass that I découpaged with insects and backed with gold paint.

The gilded vases were the perfect material to use because they were curved like the body and uniquely attractive. The breasts and bottom were particularly round and it was important to follow those curves, so that the mosaic would be 'caressable'.

I used a small rose-covered vase and drew on a bikini to define the boundaries. The rest of the body has a multitude of golds, many insects and the odd leaf but I kept away from the florals so that the bikini line was emphasised.

Opposite is a collection of materials I used and shows how much fun it is to gather up all of your product and arrange and play with it before you even begin your mosaic. The pieces in the foreground are découpaged fragments of glass with gold leaf surrounding the image. I also included antique buttons in the mosaic.

The bust had no base and needed stabilising, so I attached her to an upside down rigid plastic bucket lid before I started.

I began mosaicing from the 'bottom'

up and had lots of fun with the rosebud crotch and the inclusion of butterflies, dragonflies, bees and ladybirds. The grout river line that imitates the string bikini and the thick line under the bust cup all come into play when the black grout is done.

By the stage that the photo bottom left was taken, I was in trouble. The adhesive I always use for interior applications is white and although it was well cleaned off below the level I needed to insert the grout into, I was getting a white shadow effect around some of the glass pieces. This was despite the fact that the back of the gilded découpage pieces have three coats of polyurethane and are well sealed, and was because the white adhesive was showing through the slightly chipped edges of each piece. There was nothing I could do except change to a clear adhesive from then on. The problem was eliminated and the black grout hides 90 percent of the shadowing.

The white adhesive would have been fine if I was going to use a white grout. The reason I used a black grout was that the base was already black. How your base and grout colour and adhesive will work together are essential considerations for any glass mosaic.

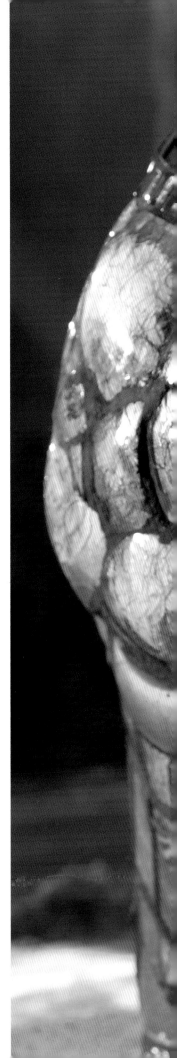

I was saving this old, **well shaped mannequin** for something special when I remembered the box of **découpaged rose vases** that were broken in transit to a market. I was really satisfied with the **challenging curves** and the green-gold richness. It is a **stunning seductive shape** and finish. Joy

Free-form flowers

Two sides of my old house were rotten and I organised a builder to reclad them. This was to be an expensive process, but as we demolished the old boards an opportunity to start with a blank canvas presented itself and to the horror of the builder I suddenly requested cement boards instead of wood. Joy

I had just completed some large-scale public art murals that were very precise and involved a lot of saw cutting, so I promised myself that this was to be organic and even nippers were forbidden. This was also the first time that I had used glass: it was cheap and I needed a lot of it. These fragments came from an art glass studio floor. I was amazed at their reflective properties. There is no light behind them, just the dark grey cement adhesive that I also used as grout.

The tiles in the background were free samples of simulated stone floor tiles. The effect I wanted to achieve was that of an old English stone cottage.

The flowers are representative of the canna lilies that surround this wall. After the constraints of commercial mosaic work, it was a delight to do a fast, fun, fantasy style job just for myself. It gave me the freedom for ideas just to evolve.

This was also the first time that I had used glass: it was cheap and I needed a lot of it.

Uncle Pete's mirror

One day my sister Caroline rocked up to my house announcing her need to make her twin, Uncle Pete, a belated 40th birthday present. He is intrigued by everything Egyptian so naturally that was our theme. Liz

When in doubt about where to start with a design, I often look to 'clip-art' style craft books for ideas. In this case our inspiration was from Eva Wilson's *Ancient Egyptian Designs for Artists and Crafts People*. We found a great shape to use as a starting point and we were off.

My 16-year-old son Lucas cut out our mirror from plywood and drilled big holes where we inserted the green and cobalt faceted glass 'gems'. (They are actually cut off the bottom of wine glasses.)

I would describe mosaic mirrors as elaborately practical and the reason I love mirror and coloured glass so much is because of its wonderful 'bling' factor. I particularly like using mirror on the edges of the ply, as the reflective qualities remind me of diamonds — a girl's best friend!

Découpaged beads (see how to do these on pages 88–89) and glass can be seen in detail in the photograph below. This mosaic was great fun and delivered the requisite 'wow' factor for Uncle Pete.

Blue glass bust

This bust is a celebration of blue — blues and greens are some of my favourite colours. It is also a great example of limiting your colour palette but not your result! Joy

The base for this bust was a readily available lightweight plastic dress shop display model. Just ensure that it is rigid enough to provide support for the mosaic.

Out of bucket-loads of art glass scraps, I found a hundred different shades of blue glass. In addition to these, I created glass shards, backed with cut-out insect images, which were then sponged with blue acrylic paint. One more accent was some vibrant blue paua (abalone) shell gift wrap paper, that I découpaged onto clear glass shards. By adding these handmade glass pieces to the other bits of glass, the mosaic reaches another level of artistic expression.

Unlike the gold bust earlier, each of the mosaic pieces I used here are flat. To ensure the bust didn't look angular, I used smaller pieces around the curves.

This bust base was black plastic, so to ensure that as much light was reflected from the mosaic as possible, I used white mastic tile glue to kill the black. I still used black grout for overall impact.

'Blue cross'

Somehow in many of my mosaics I always seem to wind up with geometric shapes and repetitive patterns, as with this blue 'cross'. Like Joy's bust opposite, I also limited my colour palette to create a very elegant and satisfying mosaic. Liz

The centre of this mosaic is a mirrored frame. I removed the stand from the back of it and used a transparent adhesive, Crystal Clear 202, to glue the crystal ornament inside the frame. I then used this crystal shape as a basis for the main 'cross' shape, which was cut out of 20 mm (¾ inch) ply.

The use of the neutrally toned, patterned refractive mirrored glass along the centre of the arms of the 'cross' creates a lovely depth to this mosaic through its contrast to the slick, chic regular mirror glass surrounding it. The grout lines further enhance the design.

Interestingly, this mosaic is only blue through its reflecting the sky in daylight. It is fascinating to watch it change through the day and into the evening.

Tone on tone, texture on texture. Refraction coupled with reflection. A dance of light in the presence of monochromatic colour.

Mosaic crosses

I really enjoy using the 'cross' shape, and even-sided crosses, in particular. Often linked with the symbolism of the number 'four', signifying wholeness and universality, to me they also represent harmony. These wall-mounted crosses can be small, satisfying and very achievable projects. The shapes have been cut from 20 mm (¾ inch) ply. The ply needs to be thick enough to glue the tricky edge pieces onto. I have used mastic glue and sanded grout on each cross. Liz

The focus of the mosaic above (left) is chopstick holders from Vietnam (which I also used, though in a different colour, in the mosaic on the next page). My sister-in-law Cynthia and I had a fantastic trip to Vietnam thanks to a young lady named Ruby and her family. They have a ceramic business over there and Cynthia and I brought back lots of treasures.

The chopstick holders surround a circle of mirror on which I have glued a Christmas ornament from 'The Trail of Painted Ponies' series. This particular horse is a mosaic pony given to me by a girlfriend. Eventually most things around our house get absorbed into a mosaic one way or another.

The fabulous images of Mexican calendar girls from the 1930s form the central theme for the next mosaic. The glass stars on which they were découpaged were end-of-season Christmas ornaments from which I nipped off the top loop. The central image is découpaged on a flat glass stand used for candles, and has a lovely raised edge that frames the image beautifully.

I then repeated the star-shaped design in the shape of the mosaic itself and through the use of red glass stars around each of the 'girls'.

Thank you to Chronicle Books and Angela Villalba for the use of these images for the découpage.

The starting inspiration for the next cross is a découpage from the outstanding art of Alphonse Mucha, created during the Art Nouveau era. Mucha had a magical way with colour which is why his art is so exciting.

I enjoy spinning off from his imagery with some quirky colour choices of my own, and some odd product choices too. Star shapes on their edges and paua, or abalone, shell tile, repeat all of the colours in the centre. The spotted shells I cut in half with my Revolution saw. My favourite colour accent of 'apple green' is in there too.

Influenced by elements of Maori design, the Kiwiana mosaic above (right) is created around a central image of a kiwi in the form of a paperweight purchased from a souvenir shop.

I really enjoy these centrally themed mosaics and liken them to decorating a room around a favourite piece, such as a Persian rug.

The red and orange radial lines out from the kiwi represent the pohutukawa flower, which is known as New Zealand's Christmas tree. The spirals are a nod to the koru, a traditional Maori symbol representing an unfurling fern frond, and are made from black polymer clay.

Découpaged glass beads Liz's way

This very simple technique will help you to make some exciting, luminous and individually different pieces. The difference between how Joy and I découpage is the material we use behind our cut-out and pasted images.

Rather than mica, polyurethane and paint, I use paper napkins (as in the mosaic right) or layers of cut-out paper patterns and images glued with P.V.A.

I use about a paintbrush approximately 25 mm (1 inch) wide and brush the back of the glass bead with slightly watered down P.V.A. glue. I then position the napkin, front-side down, on the bead and smooth it on carefully. Tear or cut around the napkin in a large circle, then turn it over to let it dry. The napkin seems to absorb any extra glue and unwanted air bubbles.

The glass beads around the centre of this Mucha-inspired cross are made in this way.

If you use a less absorbent paper image behind a piece of glass or a glass bead surface remember to carefully rub the back of the image in a radial pattern, out from the centre,

to eliminate air bubbles that can affect the image once it is dry, because it will appear shiny and not connected to the glass.

Once the bead is dry, cut the napkin closely around the edge of the bead so it is ready to mosaic.

The thickness of the glass bead creates depth and dimension and I

believe it would also protect the napkin design from fading. Other glass beads that I have made are used in Uncle Pete's mirror (page 83) and Freedom River fiesta (pages 92–93). For my rocking horse (page 132), I put skeletal leaves between the bead and the red paper backing and used it as a focal point for the spirals on the haunches of the horse.

This mosaic is all about contrast – whatever is palest or lightest will come forward from the darker, richer background and 'pop' out.

Mucha had a magical way with colour, which is why his art is so exciting.

creating with pebbles, rocks & shells

Pebbles, rocks and shells reflect nature's beauty and elements of the earth. Textural, diverse and ancient, they are nature's little gifts that can be used as the central theme of your mosaic or as an extra decorative touch. Dyed stones extend the colour palette.

Freedom River fiesta

This non-grouted mosaic features pebbles, stones and shells, as well as coloured mirrored glass, beads — in fact anything I could lay my hands on! As in this case, mosaics can record memories of places and experiences at the time when you collected the materials.

Freedom River was inspired by a trip Joy and I made to Phoenix, Arizona to attend the Society of American Mosaic Artists (SAMA) conference. The work of Ivana, an 80-year-old mosaic artist from Israel, really resonated with me. She does not grout her work and she uses a lot of stones as her background 'tile'.

Most of the materials in this piece were purchased at the conference. At the time, many artists at the conference liked using smalti, Italian-styled glass blocks. I wasn't able to buy as many as I would have liked due to the weight (I had to get them back to New Zealand), but I used what little I had in this mosaic. Liz

The **progress of this mosaic** can be seen opposite — I began with **spirals and some featured elements** and then filled it in.

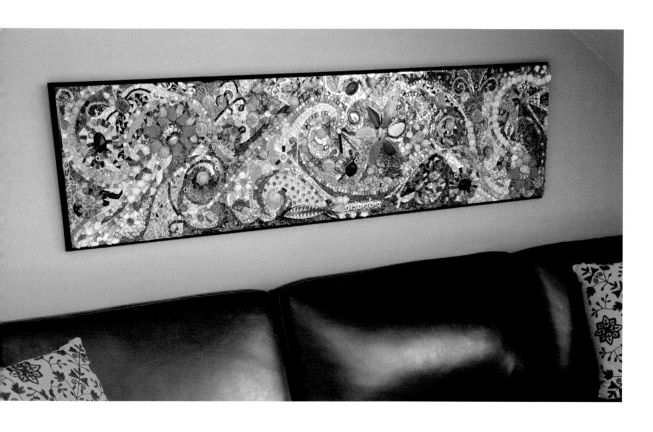

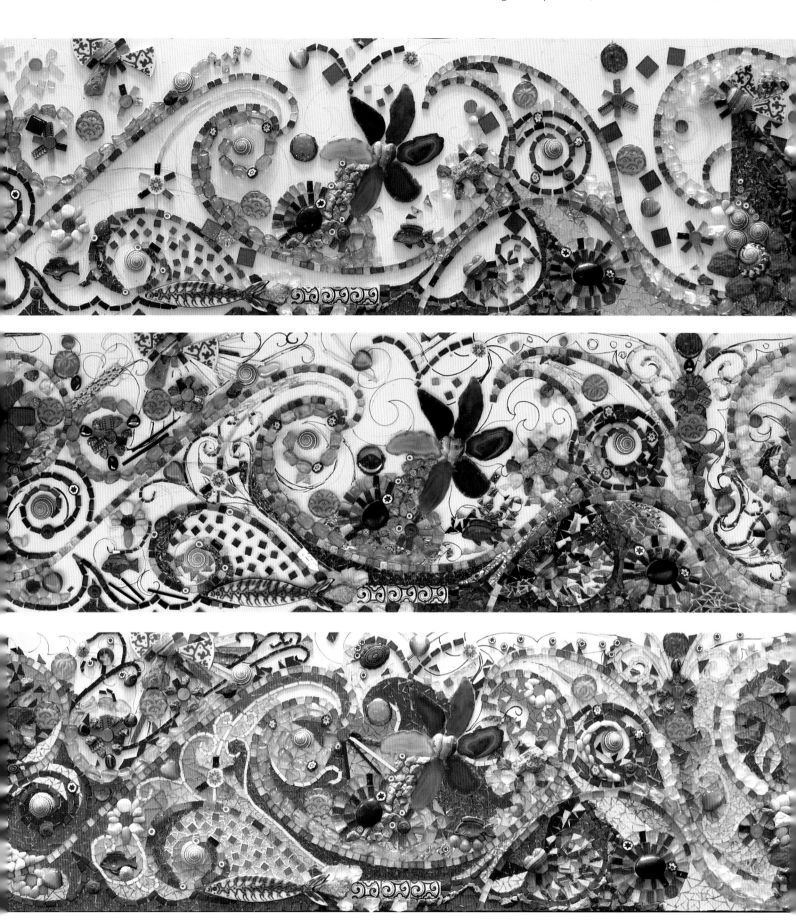

Symbology as inspiration

Symbols have different meanings and evoke different emotions for different people. They are intertwined within our world view of life. I am constantly inspired by them. The 'Om' mosaics right and opposite bless my sister-in-law Cynthia's property. The 'Om' is central to Hinduism and signifies the merging of the physical being with the spiritual. Liz

This take on the 'Om' symbol was created directly onto this outside wall by Penny Rolfe.

If you can think of it . . . then **you can create it.** There are really **no rules to mosaicing,** only a licence to experiment. **Why be ordinary?** Use a little of anything and everything!

Naturally coloured stones and pebbles create a lovely peaceful aspect to a mosaic. They are also very hard-wearing materials and are ideal for both outdoor and indoor mosaics. I think they work particularly well with strong, simple designs.

The horse head graphic that I used to create the outdoor mosaic on the next page is one of my favourite designs of all time. It is the very distinctive and very special logo of a New Zealand vineyard, Ngatarawa, www.ngatarawa.co.nz. With special permission from Alwyn Corban, I was allowed to mosaic the design. The other person who needs to be thanked and acknowledged here is Elizabeth Fuller.

She is the creator of this image and has continued her career as an illustrator, focusing on children's books.

I graduated the colours in travertine (a type of limestone) in order to spice up the neutral tones. All of the big curves were cut with the Gemini Revolution ring saw, but the eye needed the precision of the Taurus saw to get the curve tight enough. Liz

creating with polymer clay

Polymer clay enables you to 'steal' objects through creating impressions of the original, as opposed to the limited supply you have of found objects. You can go to a friend's house, take an impression from a treasured ornament, bake it in the oven and from then on you have a reusable mould. This gives you wonderful creative scope, as you can see from the pieces on this and the following pages. Let your imagination run wild!

Unlimited creativity

Prior to meeting Laurie Mika at a SAMA conference, I was exploring the mould-making possibilities of plaster. I would use polymer clay to make the mould and then pour plaster reliefs, which were then protected with resin after being painted. Laurie makes beautiful 'mosaicons' and her work inspired me to impress directly into the polymer clay with rubber stamps and small items such as keys, bug brooches and ornate relief objects. Joy

Laurie also uses a lot of metallic finishes, such as gold leaf and mica powders, which transform the polymer clay into something that looks like metal.

Polymer clay can be indented with text, jewellery bits, glass, stones and metal buttons, and then fired in the oven (according to the manufacturer's instructions). You can both make impressions with objects you want to keep and embed objects you want to use. If the object you want to use is metal, glass or china bake it in the oven with the clay and, when cooled, try to flick it out. If it comes out, glue the object in place. Some will stay in and not need gluing.

If you are using plastic objects, bake with the indentation only (you must remove the plastic object or it will melt), but then glue the plastic object back in place when the clay is baked.

I use polymer clay in so many ways. It carries 'information' from the object you impress into it with amazing detail. I make moulds from objects using the polymer clay (see page 126 in the step-by-step projects section for a description of how this is done). You can then dust the inside of the mould with talcum powder (the talcum powder will help it to release cleanly) and firmly push in softened polymer clay to transfer the detail.

Dust this form with a bronze powder and fire in the oven if you want a bronze look. Or paint it and apply gold mica powder.

This technique works well if you just need the relief of the object (not a 3D version) and can accept a flat back. All my moulds have flat backs because they get glued to frames or into trays. Mould-making becomes difficult when you want to go all around the object as you then have to create two moulds. (I never do this.)

The baked mould is reusable so you can create a wonderful resource for future projects.

Baked polymer clay does not need sealing. I have used baked polymer clay in my outdoor mosaics and after five years they have not faded. If you apply the mica powder before baking it will also not need sealing (though after five years outside the mica powder highlights seem to be disappearing). If you use gold leaf sheets on clay and then bake it, as I do in the step-by-step picture frame project on page 125, it is wise to seal them afterwards. And if you paint baked clay with acrylic paints, it is essential to use a sealer.

There are lots of exciting ways to use polymer clay and I've described just some of them on these pages next to the specific mosaics.

Tree of Life features polymer clay in many guises and a bed of china flowers.

TIP

Grout is not kind to polymer clay, so don't use it. You can manipulate the shape of the mosaic elements so they butt up tightly to each other and so eliminate the need to grout altogether.

Death of a Dream implies the end of a relationship and in the centre is a large cemetery angel. My decision to make her in plaster was that it is easy to 'antique' porous plaster and with a light wash to make it look like stone. I also moulded the wings, birds, bridal skeletons (from Mexico) and sacred heart, and used dried lichen to bed these objects into this deep tray. I then poured in the two-pot resin to seal and secure. I love the tone on tone of these creamy greens — it lends a wonderful ethereal feel.

Pride features a peacock made by hand with polymer clay and the help of a wing mould. I used brown and blue polymer clay for the bird and highlighted this with mica powder for a great shimmery effect. The eyes on the tail feathers were made in a skinny sausage of gold, brown and blue clay, which was then sliced.

The climber is reverse découpage flowers behind glass cut to shape and green polymer clay for the leaves and vine. (I would have cut china flowers from a plate, but I didn't have anything suitable at the time.)

The brickwork was stamped out onto rolled out squares of beige polymer clay with a baked clay stamp that I made for the purpose.

The whole assemblage was glued with construction adhesive onto the glass. Behind the glass I reverse découpaged an intricately cut wisteria and behind that a piece of old mirror, which reflects the sky. I firmly boarded up the back and with heat-set ink used stamps to decorate the frame.

Time Flies is centred around an old clock face with many references to flying and time throughout the work. The polymer clay has been impressed with various insects, ornaments and jewellery, as well as clock parts. I used an old picture frame with its original gold mount, which I kept under the glass. I glued all the parts I made on top of the glass with Crystal Clear 202. No grout was needed. I also incorporated some reverse découpage insects (see page 78) and used moulds for the wings (see page 126 for how to create moulds). The gold mount works well as it offers relief from the intensity of the rest of the pieces.

Waste Not, Want Not was inspired by a Victorian platter which featured these very words. Because the words were embossed (i.e., pushed out from the back of the platter), I could simply press two ribbons of polymer clay into the mould and copy the text the right way around. (A lot of old metal objects have fine detail stamped from behind, making it easy to take moulds.)

I baked the polymer clay ribbons in the metal tray so that it would harden into the same oval shape as the edge of the tray.

I used pieces of kitchenalia (Victorian miniatures of kitchen equipment made as children's toys) to take a mould from with the polymer clay.

Leaving the clay unbaked, I poured a small amount of plaster to make a flat-backed mould. When the plaster is dry, I can then remove the finished plaster object and use the polymer clay again to create a mould for the next one-off object.

The jug, cup, purse, bread and coin case are all painted plaster that was then sealed with a liberal coating of polyurethane. The rest of the pieces are a pen nib, thimble, watch, charms and collar stud. All were glued into place with Crystal Clear 202.

In the piece opposite, I captured the likeness of my friend Jesse in a box and called my creation Old King Cole, because Jesse is a 'merry old soul'. It was all just an excuse to get inventive with the finery... the ermine fur and the general 'OTTness' you can indulge in with polymer clay.

I used 15 photos of Jesse to get a likeness. My first step was to make a skull in relief, that is with a flat back, complete with teeth and eye sockets. Once I had that baked, I then made his eyeballs, baked them and put them in the sockets. This preparation enabled me to push really hard with my fingers when I formed the flesh-coloured clay into a realistic face. It was a lot of fun.

The big challenge for me on this piece was to get the polymer clay and make it look like metal, wood, flesh or fabric. It is such a playful substance — just begging for experimentation. You can either create mosaics purely from polymer clay or use it to add special features to more traditional mosaics. There are infinite possibilities for expression.

Animal Farm ('four legs good, two legs bad') was made by taking small plaster moulds from old toy animals. After painting, I arranged the animals on a small, square plate with a bark-rim design. I then poured two-pot resin over the positioned animals. It was a very easy technique — the plaster was well sealed in the resin, the animals were stuck in place and the plate provided a nice background. There were two things I didn't anticipate: there was too much reflection for my liking in this piece of whimsy — it looks fine on pale or gold objects but on darker ones the detail is lost and the shine detracts from the work; and three years on the whole resin assemblage, complete with its barbed wire hanger, parted company with the plate. It happened spontaneously and I wouldn't know how to repeat it. The effect is great, as the assemblage now hangs in a window looking like the 'suspended animation' it is.

Golden Winged Angel is made from moulds of vintage pieces, two Art Nouveau plaques, a coin, a pottery nun's head and the angel wings. The plaques and coins are painted plaster and the wings and head are polymer clay (as is the hanging crucifix). Any object that stands proud of the frame needs to be very hard, and even well-sealed plaster is not hard enough. The polymer clay is strong enough for the job, but it is not as economical as plaster, which is why I use both in my mosaics. The other consideration is that it is much easier to paint plaster. So with polymer clay I tend to use it in the colour I require and just dust it with bronze or gold mica powder.

I used a two-pot resin to seal the mosiac and secured it into an old black lacquer tray. (This work should stay in the tray as the sides are acute, unlike the plate in *Animal Farm*, which had sloping edges.)

I use the clay in so many ways. It carries 'information' from the object you impress into it with amazing detail.

Two wonderful examples of **the beautiful detail and variety of colours and effects** you can create with polymer clay.

The photograph opposite shows what I call the Bark Woman. I used polymer clay to hand-form her hands and the bird she holds. I cut out the flowers in her skirt from china plates and pushed them into green polymer clay panels (the maximum size dictated by my oven) and baked them together.

Her face was taken from a Victorian child's death mask. They would take a plaster cast of the face and this became a mould for a fired clay version. The original of this lovely smiling face is on my kitchen wall. To make the polymer clay version, I kneaded a large slab of polymer clay and dusted the mask with talcum powder (which works as a release agent), and then squashed the thick slab over it. I pushed my fingers firmly all over the features of the face, massaging the clay in. On removal, I had a mould, which I then baked in the oven so I could use it again. The mould has to be reasonably thick clay otherwise it will crack when you push the next lot of clay firmly into it.

With another dusting of talcum powder inside the mould, I then pushed a second slab of softened brown polymer clay into it, being careful to get the nose indent, eyes and mouth before removing. If you are not happy with the copy you take, ball up the clay and do it again — only bake what gives you the detail and shape you require.

I then highlighted the face with bronze mica powder and baked it.

I made a **mould from the bark of a tree** in my garden and created her body. I took impressions from a leaf **brooch** to create the **leaves** for the **hair**.

creating with
found objects

+

Found objects are great, until they run out. But life is short and they should be used. I used to own an antique store, so as you can imagine I have a shed full of found objects but I am always on the look out for more. Thrift stores, garage sales, friends, even beachcombing can yield discarded treasures, the smaller the better. Usually I look for metal items like buttons, bits of jewellery, chains, keys, dolls' limbs, dice and lead type.

My spotted unicorn

Recycling creatively is exciting! The fabulous speckled glass I used for this mosaic is the remnant of a beautiful designer jug I received as a wedding present. Unfortunately, it broke — boo hoo, tee hee! (Mosaic artists must be the only people that don't necessarily get too upset when a fine piece of china breaks!) Liz

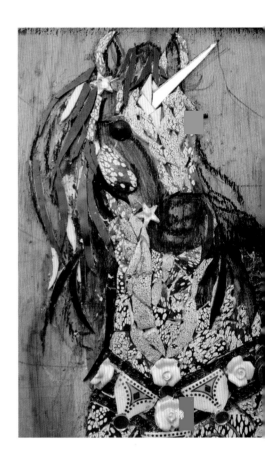

As well as the beautiful speckled glass, I went looking for other objects to suit my plans and it is easy to understand how stimulating this process is. The roses are nipped off a flower pot; I cut the stone love hearts through the middle, but you do need to take care that they do not crumble; the mirrored glass is delicious; and the red and gold patterned cups were stolen from a girlfriend (in true pique assiette fashion!). Included in the mix are also coins, beads and stars taken off napkin rings.

On the right, you can see the assembly process directly onto the ply. My sketch is fairly rough and I use it as a guide only. I like to go with the mosaicing flow, which does get a little 'touch and go', but somehow it all works out. Just remember that the viewer's eye needs to swirl around the image evenly without seeing anything foreign or jolting.

Grouted v. non-grouted

There is not a huge difference between the non-grouted (right) and grouted (far right) versions of this unicorn except that the non-grouted version looks lighter overall and lacks the definition the black grout provides. In my experience, black grout works best with pieces where clear mirror is dominant. As with my rocking horse (page 132), I used Mapei grout. It is ideal for interior mosaics as it has good colour intensity. It does dry quickly, though, so don't linger if you are grouting the whole piece, or take more time and grout in sections.

Grout rivers

Grout 'rivers' are the lines of grout created around the mosaic pieces, and they can work for you or against you. You need to watch out for them, especially in random mosaics. A lovely design can be spoiled by a line of grout catching the eye and breaking up the pattern. In contrast, in the case of this unicorn, I used the grout rivers to draw with.

While flicking through Lee J. Ames' book *Draw 50 Horses*, I noticed that an elongated cicular shape was drawn to create the joints, so I did the same with the glass. The curved background lines behind the horse were intended to help create the illusion of perspective.

GROUTING TIP

Try to govern or control the grout 'river' — the lines of grout around your mosaic pieces. You need to dictate the line.

Memory tray

I made a series of 'memory trays' — time capsules in resin. The key is to include things that are significant to a particular person's life... things from childhood like badges, charms, even tiny ornaments, or they can be found objects that signify someone's lifestyle or career — keys, bits from watches, pens, stick pins. Joy

A two-pot resin sets them in place, either completely submerged or with some poking out. They can be set into metal or wooden (even plastic) trays that are watertight and can then be wall-mounted.

When using resin, be sure to follow the instructions when mixing. I use the 30-minute variety (some set in 5 minutes). As long as your tray is watertight, you can use many materials — plastic, thick glass, metal, wood, china, paper-mache.

The pieces will move about when you pour the resin, so just reposition them. Watch out for air bubbles that will come up from under the objects. You have 30 minutes to chase them to the edge of the tray, where they will disappear. Use a toothpick to do this, and ensure you gave good ventilation when working with resins.

Random yet **balanced mosaics** are quite **tricky to achieve.** The best way I have managed **to create** **this balance** is to **prepare a lot of the product** (what you use in your mosaic) in advance and **then divide the mosaic** and the **materials into equal sections.**

Large mirror frame

I really enjoy expanding the list of products that I can incorporate into a mosaic. There really are no rules or limitations to creating mosaics. Liz

Black-lined angel plates, oval mirrors, miniature Spode plates, mother of pearl shells, flying silver herons, iridescent beads, glass snowflake Christmas ornaments, opaque rocks, silver spirals, white bird salt and pepper shakers, many tones of silver, textured mirrored glass, dove-shaped chopstick holders, white and cream Italian plates, Roman goddesses and Pan's flutes, textured plates, elongated white spiral shells, raised angel faces, enquiring white birds, black stone and vintage crystal drops – phew! – this mosaic was a found object dream.

This list sounds a lot, but be aware that there needs to be a lot more product than you initially imagine. This type of 'found object' mosaic just seems to gobble product, and if you want balance you'll need to make sure key elements of shape and/or colour appear throughout

the frame – 'random' takes planning!

For a project of this size, standing your mosaic on an easel can give you the perspective to see if your design is working or that key pieces are true and balanced. It also prevents neck pain from intense, concentrated work over a table.

For this mosaic, I prepared the frame by first painting it with black paint, then crackle medium, and finally white paint. I then used a few coats of sealer, which is very important if the frame is going into a moist environment such as a bathroom.

Once I was happy with the seal, I glued in what I call the 'exciting material'. Placing the background tiles is a lot less stimulating even though it requires the same detailed planning as the key elements. I find that having the areas divided into smaller sections helps the psyche.

Once you have glued everything, you can grout. The photos opposite show the progression from organising material and assembly to gluing and grouting. You can see how changing the colour of the grout could change the whole vibe of this piece.

Creating a beautiful object such as this mirror frame becomes a great focal point for decorating a room — it adds an unexpected twist and lots of personality to a little room — and mosaics are ideal for bathrooms or wet area environments.

Jesse's box

The base of this box was a damaged Regency tea caddy. The glass body had a crack down one side and so the caddy was rendered worthless — the perfect object to mosaic! Joy

This beautiful little tea caddy had so much to offer. Not only was it an interesting shape and design, there was also an opportunity to have light come through the sides of the box as I would be using transparent glue on glass. Because of this, I chose agate slices for the centre, front and back. When the box is displayed with light coming through from behind, the glorious blue of the agate is illuminated.

I opted for my favourite colour combination of blues and greens and I used lots of material that I had gathered on my first trip to a SAMA conference. (Liz used the treasures she gathered from this trip to create Freedom River fiesta (see also pages 92–93). It is a wonderful way to remember a good time!)

As well as the agate, I used pyrite (also known as fool's gold), glass buttons and glass tiles. I used polymer clay for the lid, embedding the buttons and creating the text that runs around the edge of the

lid ('memories are what you make them') before baking in the oven. I managed to work around the original ornamentation, leaving the feet, side scrolls and ivory knob.

I had failed to sell this box for $20 when I had my antique store, so remember to call into such places and ask if they have any broken objects as well as the more usual cracked or damaged china. You will gain huge satisfaction in bringing something back to life while creating a unique piece of art; it is a wonderful marriage of the old and the new.

The satisfaction is that you bring something back to life while creating a unique piece of art.

Nana Jeff's memory vase

Traditionally, when they made memory jars it was more like salvaging than recycling — there was pride and satisfaction in frugal times in giving something new life. My grandma salvaged a tragedy by recreating something she had loved into something new that she could love. Mosaicing can turn a negative into a positive. Liz

About 70 years ago, my grandma's old farmhouse was replaced with a new homestead. It was built in the next paddock, and the day of the move it was all hands on deck to help shift the household.

Nana Jeff's treasured Royal Doulton tea set was safely ensconced in the china cabinet. It was seldom used – and definitely only for special occasions. For reasons that we'll never know, the menfolk convinced her that they could safely carry the china cabinet and its contents without emptying it. It must have been hard for Nana Jeff to watch...

Needless to say, the Royal Doulton tea set did not survive intact. However, Nana Jeff gathered up the pieces, found a large preserving jar and some putty out of the shed and pushed the pretty rose-patterned pieces onto the jar, creating a beautiful vase.

American memory jugs were a similar tradition. In the late 1800s, it was popular for American women to gather together domestic souvenirs such as keys, bits of broken dolls and ornaments, buttons, jewellery, thimbles and other tokens of their everyday lives. Discarded vessels such as jugs, jars or vases were thickly covered with putty and the objects well embedded. Usually the putty was then disguised with bronze paint.

Today, some authentic examples of these memory jugs can be found in museums. What a wonderful example of both the 'waste not, want not' mentality of these women and the desire in all of us to decorate our homes. Some possessions just have too many memories to discard them, even when they are damaged.

Other early examples of this type of 'found object' mosaic include Victorian shell art, where shells collected at the beach were used to decorate box lids. What better way to commemorate a trip to the seaside?

Crazy quilts were another example of 'mosaic' art that incorporated the frugal habit of keeping scraps of cloth and using them to create something beautiful. The most wonderful examples have richly coloured scraps of velvet and satin embroidered together with ornate stitches on top of which more ornate embroidery embellished and personalised the quilt.

The common thread in all these examples is that we can all make something exquisite out of the ordinary.

This wonderful mosaic is Joy's Homage to Memory Vases. Most of the elements were created using moulds and then painted to give a Victorian feel. Joy used construction adhesive rather than the traditional putty (which can take up to a year to cure), and a white grout to keep the 'soft' look.

Other early examples of traditional mosaics include Victorian shell art, where shells collected at the beach were used to decorate box lids. What better way to commemorate a trip to the seaside?

The horned dragon – Seranox

My middle son Alexander's passion is with animation and fanciful characters. He was drawing dragons one day and I remarked that a dragon would be fun to mosaic, so Alex enlarged his design onto some plywood. It was cut out with a jigsaw and screwed to the studs in the wall of my office, its final destination. Liz

With certain pieces, like Seranox, I screw the substructure to the wall — you can treat the work like a painting and step back to see if it is working. But remember that as you glue more material on, your mosaic can get very heavy so use some serious screws to hold it on the wall. If you want to be able to take the mosaic down, don't glue or grout the pieces of the mosaic that cover the screw holes. After you have grouted the mosaic, you can just stick these pieces in place with Blu Tack (or equivalent). If you need to remove the whole mosaic, you find your loose pieces and remove them to access the screws.

Seranox is a real 'found' objects project in that I went into all my materials left over from other projects and just selected what I thought would look good together. I sourced from dyed rocks, 1960s plates, paua or abalone shell, glass beads and mirrored glass, Italian tiles, chop stick holders from Vietnam, silver ball beads and shell spirals inserted in a turquoise plastic plate!

It is one of those projects that you begin with no real direction and halfway through you think… this thing is huge and really quite complicated! So much of the product is being stacked up on itself and the mirror cutting for the wings takes time.

Often a mosaic at this stage just sits half finished for about a year or so, especially if I loose my flow from the interruptions of life. In order to get back into 'the creative groove', I almost have to 'brace myself' for the challenge again in order to get motivated. Just one of my challenges with Seranox was to differentiate the top and the underside of his wings and arms.

I was particularly pleased with the contoured glass that I used to create the ridged texture of the horns. I also like using 'teddy bear' eyes for the creatures I create. In this case it seems particularly odd to have a big, muscular, powerful dragon sporting 'teddy bear' eyes! But it works!

It is a fun thing to create with your children. Alex is extremely clever with his fanciful designs and we both enjoy exploring the worlds of symbology and mythology.

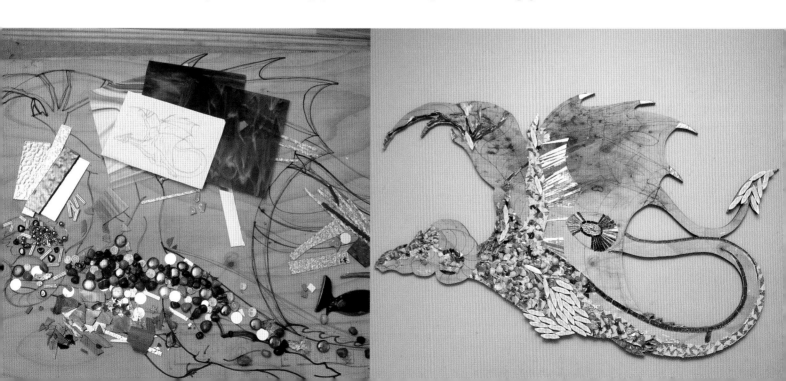

The following pages take you through five projects — beginning with a very simple photo frame. You can follow the 'recipe' closely or use it as a springboard for your own creativity. The main thing is to get started and have a go playing with the material. Your skills at gluing and grouting will improve as you go and you'll discover your own preferences. However, we hope that our mistakes will save you time and money — we've included where things went wrong so you can avoid those pitfalls.

Easy frame

This is a great first project and by using pre-cut glass tiles no tools are needed.

What you need

- Photo frame with a flat frame surface, approximately 20 cm x 25 cm (8 inch x 10 inch)
- Pre-cut glass tile (greens)
- Glass glitter squares (green)
- 5 buttons for corners and top centre (optional)
- Black cord (the thickness will be based on the gap between the outer and inner tile borders)
- P.V.A. glue (wood or craft glue). For glass to plastic, or glass to wood I used P.V.A. and for the buttons a blob of two-pot Araldite.

1 The first step is to find a suitable frame. You will need one with a flat surface. I chose a dark plastic frame and was lucky enough to find one that had a handy little raised edge around the outside, so there was no exposed edge on the finished frame.

2 I decided on emerald green and gold as my colour palette. Tile shops sell the larger squares used on the outer edge, and the smaller glitter squares are sold in craft shops. Work out how many you need for your frame — be generous as you don't want to run out. You can always use leftovers for other projects.

3 You will also need to gauge the thickness of the black cord so that it fills any gaps between your inside and outside border. It will look smart and it means you don't need to grout!

4 When you have everything assembled and have placed all the tiles and cord to make sure everything fits and looks good, start gluing the outside tiles around the frame. Work carefully with the glue using a toothpick as this will avoid having to clean up any glue at the next stage.

5 Glue the inside tiles in the same way and then glue in your black cord so that the two rows of tiles are snug together.

6 If using buttons, add them now, or your own decorative additions to the corners.

Remember to use a different adhesive from the P.V.A. as you are gluing onto glass tiles.

7 Clean off any excess glue with a toothpick. Leave to dry overnight and then you are ready to add a photo, or quotation or... if you want to take this project to the next level and play with some polymer clay — read on!

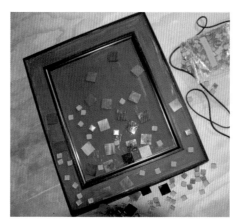

1 Photo frame with scattering of glass tiles and black cord. Assemble your mosaic before you start gluing so that you know everything fits snugly.

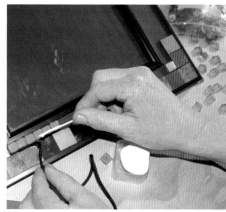

2 Glue the tiles around the edge of the frame with P.V.A. Then glue the black cord between the rows of tiles instead of using grout.

Taking your frame further

If you want to take the frame a step further, try using polymer clay to create a beautiful artwork. The central theme I chose was 'eternal love', and with this in mind I looked for relevant objects to use or borrow. Keep the objects small and restrict your colour palette.

What you need

- Polymer clay (green, brown, white and gold)
- Gold leaf sheets (which are backed with tissue paper)
- Bronze and gold mica powder and paintbrush
- Jewellery bits and buttons used direct
- Jewellery bits and charms to make impressions in the clay
- Rubber stamps (if using)
- Flat knife, craft knife
- Rolling pin
- Baking paper
- Talcum powder
- Central plaque to take a mould from
- Acrylic paint for the central plaque
- Sealer for the painted central plaque and the gold leaf
- Black paper to place behind the glass
- Construction adhesive, which may seem like overkill for a small indoor mosaic but I like to use it as a firm base to embed the different materials. Alternatively, you could use Crystal Clear 202 (which Liz uses frequently) but it can seem a little too flexible when dry and give pieces a disconcerting 'bounce'.

Complementary green polymer clay tiles can be impressed with rubber stamps (some stamps don't like the gold leaf). Hearts, anchors, crosses, buttons and jewellery bits can be used. Prepare the clay the same way, aim for a consistent thickness and always use the baking sheet as the clay sticks.

The first steps in this project are to create the different elements you want to use in the mosaic. I began with the central plaque of the 'kissing lovers' and created a reusable mould. This technique can be applied to any object you want to take a mould from.

Creating a mould

1 Dust the original plaque with talcum powder (for easy release). Warm up the polymer clay by squeezing in your hands for a few minutes. (Any colour clay is fine as this is your mould, not the finished piece that will be used in the mosaic.) Make a ball, flatten it to approximately 8 mm (0.3 inch) thick and press firmly onto the plaque so you get a good impression. Repeat the process if you are not satisfied. Once you are happy with the result, bake the polymer clay in the oven to the manufacturer's instructions. You now have a reusable mould.

Creating the final piece for the mosaic

2 Dust the inside of your mould with talcum powder. After warming the white polymer clay, flatten into a slab 4–5 mm (0.15–0.2 inch) thick and press firmly into the mould. Bake to set and then experiment with paint techniques. I used a light wash of the acrylic paint over the white clay plaque and then rubbed off the highlights with a rag to give an 'antiqued' effect. You can also rub some gold paint on the high points with your finger. Once you have the look that you want, seal it. [Photo 1]

Creating the gold leaf impressions

3 Take a sheet of baking paper and roll out the green clay to 4–5 mm (0.15–0.2 inch) thick and slightly larger than the gold sheet. Carefully place the gold sheet, which is sold backed with tissue paper, onto the clay. Leave the tissue on while you smooth the gold onto the clay with your fingers. Then, gently lift a corner of the tissue to see if a bond has formed and remove the tissue when it has. [Photo 2]

4 Trim the edges around the sheet and you have your gold leaf clay ready to use. Anticipating the size of the final pieces, cut the gilded clay into squares, rectangles, triangles and thin strips (these will be used instead of grout).

5 Before you start making the impressions into the gilded clay, experiment on the green clay, which you can reject and reuse if you make a mistake. When you make an impression into the gilded clay, use firm pressure; be deliberate, don't 'rock and roll'. By pressing down with an object the squared-off soft gilded clay will bulge and you will need to square it off again before baking.

6 Set aside the tiles and when you have made all the pieces, bake in one batch. Seal. [Photos 3 and 4]

Creating the green and gold tiles

7 Prepare the green and gold clay the same way as for the previous steps. Aim for a consistent thickness (4–5 mm/0.15–0.2 inch) and always use the baking sheet, as the clay sticks. Once you have the pieces cut to size, you can impress them — hearts, anchors, crosses, buttons and jewellery bits can all be used. As they may get distorted during handling, be sure to square them off with your knife before baking. A delicate dusting of gold mica powder will highlight the detail. No sealing is needed after baking these pieces.

The frame around the central plaque has been made using brown polymer clay. I rolled out the clay and then pressed the plaque down hard into it and cut out the circle it created so that the plaque could be embedded. You could then impress a design onto the frame before baking. I found some fancy metal corners from the cover of an old book and pushed them into the clay. Finally, I highlighted the frame with bronze and gold mica powder and baked the whole thing. [Photo 5]

Assembly

8 To assemble, start with the four corners and the centre, then fill in with the pieces you have created. Have some extra tiles to hand so that you can choose what looks or fits best. Ideally, all the pieces will fit snugly together. If there is a tricky area, you can make a specific tile to fix the problem. You can also use the thin gold-leafed strips you made earlier. These can be simply cut to length with a craft knife and the tiles can be shaved into shape. At this point you can place your extra jewellery bits and buttons. [Photo 6]

Gluing

9 Put black paper behind the glass before you start gluing and make sure the mosaic fits perfectly. Use a thick adhesive that is easy to control and allows you to level the tiles as you go.

This process is fun, addictive and will bring out your inner child!

1 Reproduce the central plaque. The blue baked polymer clay is the mould taken from the old round brass box. The white clay impression is then baked and painted as shown.

2 Apply gold leaf to the rolled out polymer clay. Cut into thin strips for grout and squares and rectangles in the final size you want to make impressions into.

3 Making the four corners from a mould of a necklace clasp.

4 Using the insect brooches to make impressions into the gilded clay.

5 Highlight your mosaic pieces with gold mica powder, but use it sparingly.

6 Assemble straight onto the glass, placing the central plaque and four corners first. Aim for balance rather than symmetry.

Turtle shell mosaic

This project was inspired by the rich, thickly glazed pottery that lies unwanted in most thrift stores. Oval metal trays for the substructure are also easily found. Turtle shells are by nature geometric and so suit being divided up and mosaiced. Black grout lines imitate the separation around the shells' shapes.

Photo: Carolyn Fears-Troadec

What you need

- ◆ 2 photocopies of your shell design, scissors, rubber cement for draughting
- ◆ Oval metal tray or serving platter (you will be gluing on the underside of the tray to get the domed shell shape)
- ◆ Lots of pottery in browns and ochre
- ◆ Tile nippers
- ◆ Construction adhesive
- ◆ Black grout

Design your mosaic

1 Based on the tray size and shape, create your design for the 'shell' and then make two photocopies of your sketch enlarged to the size of the tray. I coloured one of the photocopies. [Photo 1]

2 Number the central sections where the shape is important on both photocopies so you can keep track of the pieces as they are cut to shape. The border pieces don't need to be numbered as they are interchangeable. [Photo 2]

Nibble your pieces to the right shapes

3 I started with the edge shapes and by using the handles of the mugs and the edges of the plates and saucers I was able to save a lot of time. For the outside edge of the shell, I found the ribbed edges of the plates worked particularly well. They look like the rim of the shell and provide a finished edge for the mosaic. [Photos 3 and 4]

4 Before you begin on the central shapes, glue the numbered pieces of paper you cut out from your photocopy onto the pottery with rubber cement. You will then have a guide to the shape and the pieces will be easy to assemble. As each piece is nibbled, put it on your template. [Photo 5]

5 When using the tile nippers, just bite into the material a little way, before applying pressure. Practise on some waste material. You can dictate a break by the angle of the

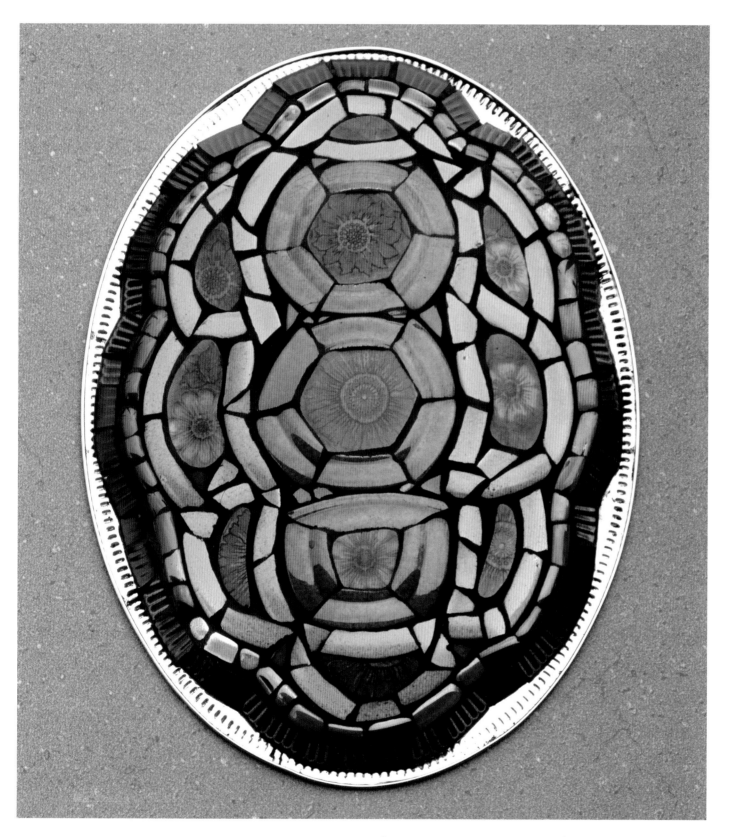

This mosaic is a great example of **bringing simplicity and impact together** through nature and pottery.

1 Enlarge your design to the size of the tray. Make two copies and colour one to show the nipped shapes and grout lines.

2 Number the shapes on both copies and cut out the black and white shapes to glue to the chosen pottery as a guide.

3 Nip the handles from the mugs, as they will make a rounded edge between the central shapes and the ribbed border.

4 Using the edges of the saucers and plates makes for less nipping and a clean, rounded edge.

5 To nip the central shapes, use your numbered template and start the nip on a straight line through the plate. Then nip clockwise around the shape.

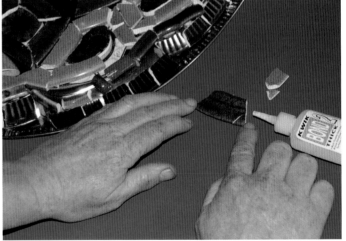

6 Glue any broken nips with ceramic adhesive right away (before you lose the pieces).

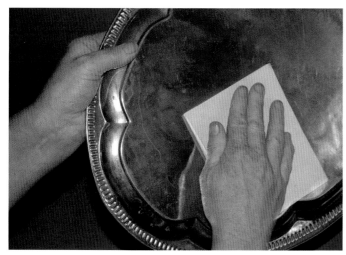

7 Prepare the metal tray by sanding off all the loose material to create a good surface for the adhesive.

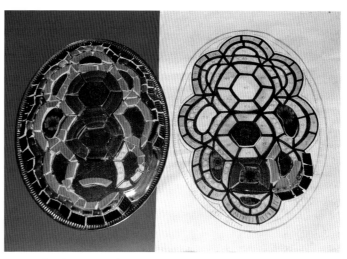

8 Transfer the pieces from the sheet to the tray. You can peel the paper guides off at this stage or after gluing.

9 Glue the pottery pieces onto the tray with construction adhesive.

10 Glued and ready for the black grout.

nippers or literally nibble your way around a shape. If you make a mistake, you can glue your 'bits' together with a ceramic adhesive. Do this right away, before you lose the small pieces. [Photo 6]

Prepare the tray
6 If you plan to hang your tray from a wall, drill two holes through the tray near the top. Twist a strong wire through these holes to form a loop behind the tray. You will see the knot as you glue, but it will eventually be hidden and secured to the tray firmly by the built-up curved shell. Be aware of the weight of the final piece

when choosing your wire. Sand the tray surface to rough it up. This will help the glue to adhere well. Remember, you are using the back of the tray to give the rounded shell shape. [Photo 7]

Assembling and gluing the pottery pieces
7 Transfer the pieces from your coloured photocopy to the tray. Once it is all assembled, peel the paper off the numbered central pieces. [Photo 8]

8 Beginning in the centre, glue the pieces in place. For this project, I've used

construction adhesive: it enables the mosaic to be hung outdoors (the tray being metal is also ideal for this), it is inexpensive and application is easy with the gun canister. Also, this adhesive is thick and so it allows me to build up the centre of the mosaic and exaggerate the roundness of the shell. [Photo 9]

Grouting
9 I left the gaps between pieces intentionally wide as the black grout was an important part of the design. Prepare the grout as per instructions and apply. Clean off and hang once cured. [Photo 10]

Rocking horse

The time had come for me to quit making mirrors for a while and work on something three dimensional. While shopping one day my eagle eyes spied this fabulous horse form. I knew that Ruth Day had worked successfully on paper-mache so now it was my turn. You could adapt this project for any paper-mache form — bust, teddy bear, box, etc.

What you need

- A suitable substructure, in this case a paper-mache rocking horse
- Large glass beads, skeletal leaves and napkins (for découpaged tesserae, see page 88 for instructions on how to make these yourself)
- A variety of mirrored glass
- Teddy bear eyes
- Some tiles for the rockers
- Stars

- Nipped roses from a plant pot
- Shell beads for the reins
- Mirrored circles
- Glass cutter and glass nippers
- P.V.A. glue
- Mastic glue
- Grout
- Expanding glue if the substructure has vulnerable points and the weight of the mosaic is likely to be too much

To tell you the truth, I prefer to work in two dimensions — I use less product and there is not the repetition created by two sides (and an underbelly!). But it was my time to stretch and grow...

I knew I wanted to use spirals as they are a great shape to break up big areas into smaller, more manageable spaces. The découpaged glass beads work really well as the centre of the spirals, as do the stars and roses, giving my horse an element of unpredictability (and they are fun to use).

Below and on the following pages is a step-by-step description of how this horse was created, including some stumbles along the way, which hopefully you can avoid if you try a similar project.

Prepare your substructure

1 If you are using a paper-mache substructure (as I have here), apply a mixture of 50:50 P.V.A. and water with a paint brush. This will seal your substructure.

This was my first stumble – I did not seal my horse... shame. I started mosaicing my merry way all over the torso and because I had not sealed it I soon realised that I had to mosaic *every* surface, including the bottom of the rockers.

2 Strengthen the substructure if you need to, that is if there are weight-bearing parts, in this case the legs and rockers. I recommend creating a nozzle-sized hole in each end of the rockers and each leg. Insert an expanding glue, such as Gorilla Glue, to strengthen the form from the inside.

This was the second lesson for me — halfway through gluing my mosaic, the rockers collapsed and my little baby had to go into horse hospital. I had to wet the rockers a little and hang the horse upside down on a pole. Once some of the former shape had returned, I had to hang it from the ceiling until I could completely mosaic and grout the rockers and lower legs. Although the horse looks perfect, under one of its rockers there is a stack of coins to balance it!

Draw your design

3 Once you have your substructure properly prepared, used a pencil to draw on your design. Remember to play with your materials and work out designs and patterns as you go. Once you are happy with your design, you can draw over it with a marker pen. With this project, I used spirals to break up the large areas. [Photo below right]

Time to glue your mosaic

4 It is very important with this project to work from the bottom up. Firstly, mosaic the rockers, then the legs (like I didn't do!). I would even carefully grout them at this stage and let them dry overnight so they are as hard as concrete and able to bear the weight of the mosaic material you glue on next. [Photo 1]

5 Work over the torso. If you want to have some symmetry, mosaic an element, such as the shoulder spiral, one side and then do the other side at each stage rather than complete a whole side. Doing this will ensure that you have enough product spread evenly around the horse. [Photo 2]

6 Place the centrepieces of your spirals; whether a china rose, découpaged glass bead, star or a mirrored circle. [Photo 3]

7 With some of my spirals, I glued the blocks of glass radiating out from the spiral line to give more texture and dynamic to the final design. [Photo 4]

8 Keep the glue contained to only the region you are working on. Use a cotton bud if necessary to clean up as you go. [Photo 5]

9 Once you have the spiral centres and lines done you can fill the spaces in between. [Photo 6]

10 Final touches. I used glass teddy bear eyes for a sense of depth and realism and experimented with tesserae for the mane and tail. [Photo 7]

11 When your horse is completely dry (leave overnight at least), you can apply the grout. I used Mapei grout as it is fabulous for mosaics – the black is really black and the other colours available, although mainly neutral, are intense and very good quality.

Play around with your materials and colours before you start; something new and unexpected always surfaces. On this project I discovered the effect of working on the spirals with the rectangles of mirror radiating out from the centre.

1 Glue your mosaic from the bottom up (not like I did). Gluing and grouting the rockers and legs gives you a solid foundation.

2 Begin gluing the torso, doing one area at a time. Remember to ensure your product is spread evenly around the horse.

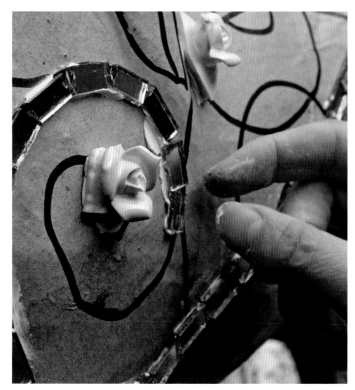

3 If you are using spiral designs, place the centrepieces first and then glue your spiral.

4 Some spirals use the glass tiles running along the spiral (gold), others have the glass radiating out from the spiral (silver).

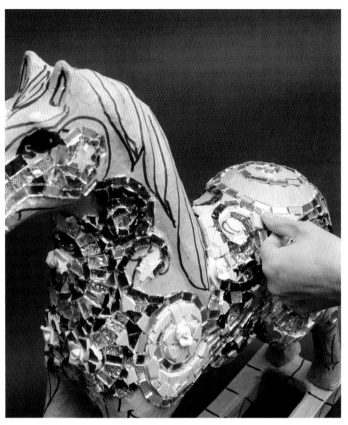

5 Glue each area as you go and keep your substructure tidy — clean the glue off with a cotton bud if necessary.

6 Once you have the spiral centres and lines done you can fill the spaces in between.

7 It's great fun working out the best way to finish details, such as the mane shown here. I used mirrored glass in long strips, which also features on the legs.

8 My finished horse awaiting grouting. Already grouted are those pesky rockers (with coins holding one side up, thankfully unseen).

Wild West horse mirror

The inspiration for this horse came after browsing through the pages of *The Carousel Animal*, a delicious book of historic carousel animals written by Tobin Fraley and photographed by Gary Sinick. Frozen in time, the richly decorated carousel animal is truly magical, somehow capturing the smiles of children at the fun fair.

What you need
- Ply to size 80 cm wide x 60 cm high (approximately 32 inch by 24 inch), 20 mm (¾ inch) thick
- Timber for the frame, or take to a frame shop
- Filler for nail holes and to neaten frame
- Paints for frame, crackle medium plus varnish
- Assorted colours of glass
- Coloured stones
- Glass beads
- Stars (the brass ones are napkin rings)
- Variety of other tesserae
- Mirror
- Glass cutters, glass pliers, mosaic glass nippers, tracing paper
- Tile glue and grout

Preparing the frame
I took the pre-cut ply to a frame store, where they made the outside frame from the timber they use for stretching canvases.

1 Use a quick-drying filler to fill the nail holes and smooth edges, then sand. [Photo 1]

2 Paint the base coat — in this case I used Burnt Umber. Once dry, generously apply crackle medium with a thicker brush. Keep the brush movement in line with the grain of the frame. Mitre the corners to maintain a neat finish. Allow a couple of hours to dry. [Photo 2]

3 Paint Burnt Sienna over the dried crackle medium. Remember to follow the grain. [Photo 3]

4 Keep adding layers of crackle medium and paint to create the frame's rich finish. I painted Light Red Oxide, crackle medium again then Burnt Sienna as I had thought this would be my final colour. However, I preferred the darker Burnt Umber so I poured the crackle medium from the bottle along the frame then spread it out evenly with my brush. (The more crackle medium the wider the cracks.)

When I painted the final coat of Burnt Umber, I did not use any water to help thin the paint and as the paint was so thick the cracks did not appear immediately. By chance, I applied some water-based varnish just before the Burnt Umber dried. The more watery consistency of the varnish instantly activated the crackle medium and I wound up with some very exciting, expressive cracks. Once dry, apply at least two more coats of varnish as that protects the frame from the process of grouting. [Photo 4]

Assemble and cut out your tesserae
5 Carefully draw your design onto the ply at some stage. You will see from

the step-by-step photos that I drew my design before I started painting and then couldn't resist mosaicing during the painting process! Consequently, I ended up with glue, mohair from clothing and chips of glass in my paint finish.

6 Lay out your colours to see what works best before you begin cutting the shapes. I cut out most of the shapes with my glass cutter and the mosaic glass nippers.

For tricky shapes like the feathers, the Indian head and the hooves, trace the design onto tracing paper. Cut it out then draw around it onto your glass or tile with a permanent marker. If you are going to use a saw such as the Gemini Taurus glass saw, put a water-resistant gel over your lines so they don't wash away while you are cutting. [Photo 5]

7 Cut or 'nibble' out all your shapes and assemble your tesserae onto the plywood before you start gluing.

The centrepiece of the saddle is an **Indian head design** based on the door handles on **the Art Deco cinema in Steamboat Springs,** Colorado. (I love those door handles!) Naturally, **turquoise stones** had to be included along with **feathers and the Indian arrow symbol.** This type of mosaic is very much like **creating a stained glass window.** Liz

Gluing your mosaic

8 I completed the horse first then I worked on the radial wedges of mirror. In between I kept adding to the outside border, but it is probably easier to do each step separately!

Enjoy the process of assembling and gluing your design, and be open to changing things as you go. Sometimes it is only when you begin that you see great combinations of colour and materials. [Photos 7 and 8]

9 I made a cardboard template of the outside border, which I used as a reference for the shape the outside edge of the pieces of mirror would be. Placing and gluing the mirror pieces took a while, so to break the monotony I started on the random pattern of glass around the outside edge. [Photos 9, 10 and 11]

10 Once the project was dry (leave at least overnight), I grouted it. I mix my grout on the dry side as too much water in the mix leaves cracks once the water has evaporated. [Photo 12]

1 Fill the nail holes in your frame and smooth the edges. Then sand ready for painting.

2 Paint on the base coat. Once dry, generously apply crackle medium with a thicker brush. Allow a couple of hours to dry.

3 Paint Burnt Sienna over the dried crackle medium. Follow the grain.

4 Layers of crackle medium and paint create the wonderful 'distressed' frame.

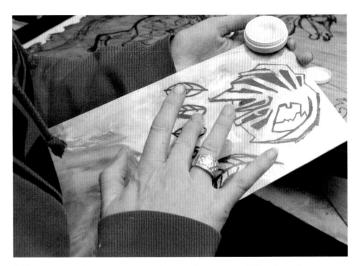

5 If you are using a saw to cut your shapes, seal the drawings on glass with a water-resistant gel.

6 Here I am using the glass saw (with its water tray, hence the need to seal my drawing) to cut out my design.

7 Have fun placing and gluing your pieces. The tail is made with fine slivers of glass.

8 My designs evolve and become more refined along the creative path.

9 This template helped me to keep the border even around the inside of the frame.

10 Use the border template to help reference your outside edge.

11 Radial lines of mirror are an effective background.

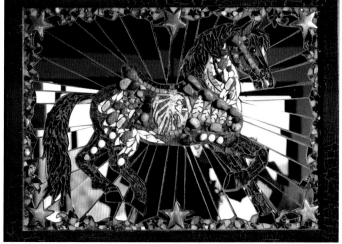

12 Varnish the frame repeatedly before and after grouting. I chose a dark grout, which is my preference with mirror mosaics.

Resources

HARDWARE STORES: For all the materials and tools such as the cement sheets, builders' adhesives, tools for construction and engraving.

TILE STORES: Tiles, tile adhesives, grout, specific tools such as nippers and scorers, hireage of tile saws. Remember to ask if there are any unwanted deleted range or sample tiles as most stores are happy to pass them on.

GLASS COMPANIES: Sell sheets of art glass or offcuts, tools and glass embellishments.

THRIFT STORES: Trays, frames, china, buttons, jewellery bits and suitable bases to mosaic over such as vases, boxes, furniture and lots more.

CRAFT STORES: Canvas, paint, adhesives, tools, rubber stamps, charms, buttons and jewellery bits.

FAMILY/FRIENDS: All their wonderful cast-offs and chipped, cracked and surplus china.

Don't forget the obvious beach glass in the sand and pebbles when you're somewhere special; being a mosaic artist is a lot like being a treasure hunter. Some things are immediately obvious as to what you will use them for and others can be stored until their time comes.

There are not many (if any) New Zealand specialist stores for mosaic materials and this has made travelling a quest for what we can't get here. If you are in a similar situation, the trips to SAMA (Society American Mosaic Artists)

annual conventions, held late March in a different city each year, have been a major source for specialist materials such as millefiori, small coloured glass sparkly squares, agates, fossils and whatever else I can cram into my suitcase. They also have demonstrations, the latest techniques, tours, workshops, speakers, presentations and an amazing marketplace.

I have listed some of the vendors here, as well as SAMA and the mosaic schools in America that have mosaic workshops.

I have been able to procure some great stuff online, including rubber stamps and even a stamp-making machine so that I can now make my own.

SOME USEFUL SUPPLIERS AND ORGANISATIONS:
Appomattox Tile Art Company — Making Marvelous Mosaics & More www.appomattoxtileart.com/aboutus.php

British Association for Modern Mosaic (BAMM) www.bamm.org.uk

The Chicago Mosaic School www.chicagomosaicschool.com

Crystaline Mosaics www.crystalinemosaics.com

Gemini Saw Company www.geminisaw.com

Home Goods www.homegoods.com

Inner Piece http://inner-piece.com

Institute of Mosaic Art, Oakland, California www.instituteofmosaicart.com

Ken Mason Tile www.kmt-bcia.com

Kneadatite http://kneadatite.com

Miami Mosaic Academy www.mosaictools.com/classes/miami

Michael's Craft Stores www.michaels.com

Mosaic Association of Australia and New Zealand (MAANZ) www.maanz.org

Mosaic Rocks! www.mosaicrocks.com

Mosaic tools www.mosaictools.com

Murano Millefiori www.muranomillefiori.com

Sauvarins Glass Studio www.sauvarinsglass.co.nz

Society of American Mosaic Artists (SAMA) www.americanmosaics.org

Wit's End Mosaic www.witsendmosaic.com

Glossary

agate a semi-precious stone (a form of quartz)

bisque a type of china or baked clay that has not been glazed

crackle medium creates an antique and decorative effect on painted surfaces

découpage decorating an object by gluing coloured paper on to it and adding paint and gilding effects

expanding glue a foaming polyurethane adhesive that expands into cavities and cracks, e.g., Gorilla Glue

gold leaf gold that has been hammered into extremely thin sheets, used for gilding

gold size adhesives used to glue gold leaf to any surface

grout a thin mortar used in the gaps between tiles, plates, glass etc. in your mosaic, can be coloured

Mapei grout a brand of grout

mastic a type of adhesive made from plant resin

mica powder finely ground minerals that add a metallic lustre

paper-mache paper mixed with glue and moulded into various shapes

pique assiette a type of mosaic using broken ceramic pieces

polymer clay a material that can be sculpted or will take impressions of other objects that is then baked hard

pyrite a mineral with a metallic lustre in shades of bronze, silver and gold (also known as 'fool's gold')

radial tile saw a circular saw which hangs from a horizontal arm for angled and square cuts; the water-cooled diamond-rimmed blade will cut tile, ceramics and glass, etc.

resin, two-pot a strong, versatile adhesive that bonds wood, metal, stone, ceramics, some plastics

ring tile saw allows you to cut curves and complicated patterns out of glass, ceramic and tile, the hardness of the material it will cut through depends on the quality of blade you are using

smalti Italian glass tile for mosaics

substructure what you glue your mosaic pieces onto

tesserae the pieces of your mosaic

tile scorer (tile scriber) used to score tiles so they snap along a straight edge

tile nippers used like pincers, nippers break off small pieces of tile allowing you to 'nibble' basic shapes

travertine form of limestone deposited by mineral springs; colour range is white to tan

This linear piece is totally inspired by the Art Deco era of the 1920s and 1930s. During this time, there was a fascination with geometric abstraction, modern mechanics and the dynamic movements created by zig zags, diagonals and radial lines.

The stylised motifs I used were inspired by the images in Eva Weber's book, *American Deco*. The top fan shape is representational of the Egyptian papyrus leaf. The découpage beneath that is of a screen designed by Paul Fehér and the image contains many Art Deco motifs including concentric arches, stylised foliage, spirals and acute chevrons. Its tone on tone quality set the scene for my interpretation of it and extension from it in this mosaic.

My juxtaposed spiral vines also create a zig zag effect. I built up the spirals on a few levels so that they interact like a freeway's under and overpasses. The leaves radiate out from the spirals and some are angled and tilted.

Elegance is achieved by the limited colour palette while contrast is created by the burnt orange tones and enhanced by the black lines. Also, I had to insert some travertine blocks to provide relief from all of the 'bling' of the coloured mirrored glass. Liz

Index